THE ECONOMICS OF GOD'S PLAN

A Mandate for Surplus Creation

William B. McKee

WESTBOW
PRESS®
A DIVISION OF THOMAS NELSON
& ZONDERVAN

WestBow Press books may be ordered through booksellers or by contacting:

WestBow Press
A Division of Thomas Nelson & Zondervan
1663 Liberty Drive
Bloomington, IN 47403
www.westbowpress.com
1 (866) 928-1240

ISBN: 978-1-9736-5795-8 (hc)
ISBN: 978-1-9736-5793-4 (e)

Library of Congress Control Number: 2019904404

Print information available on the last page.

WestBow Press rev. date: 4/15/2019

CONTENTS

THE ECONOMICS OF GOD'S PLAN

THE ECONOMICS OF GOD'S PLAN

A Mandate for **Surplus** Creation

William B. McKee

Bachelor of Science—USAFA
Master of Arts—Economics—UCLA
Master of Theology—Fuller Seminary

ACKNOWLEDGMENTS

Thanks to my wife, Penne, for supporting me in this new adventure—*and for softening my heart.*

Thanks to all my brothers and sisters in Christ, who have been encouragers and given their time. No one was more generous than Reverend Robert Felix, MDiv. His thoughts and contributions were invaluable as a pastor to the rising generations.

PREFACE

Even to your old age I am he,
even when you turn gray I will carry you.
I have made, and I will bear;
I will carry and will save.

—Isaiah 46:4 (NRSV)

I formulated the thesis for this book over five years ago, while I was still in my sixties. I have engaged on the issue of economics and theology with some very special and bright people along the way, including Dr. Michael Moore, Fuller Seminary; Dr. Leighton Ford, Leighton Ford Ministries; and Dr. David Brown, Princeton University.

I was born a type A personality. Prayerfully, that has moderated a bit in the last several years as I have come to accept life is not about me. I have been competitive and goal-oriented. It has been on display throughout my life in business and sports. My life has been an interesting journey with experience as a USAF interceptor pilot, commercial banker, associate economics professor, venture capitalist, securities underwriter, and board member of public and private companies. I then became a seminarian and finally an adult Christian educator.

I think God speaks through everyday people. When we hear His voice through them, our lives are guided and changed. Scripture calls such people מַלְאָך (mal·'āḵ) in Hebrew and ἄγγελος (ang'-el-os) in Greek. Both words mean messenger, but with a divine purpose. They are sometimes referred to as angels. Looking back, I see a number of angels who intervened in my life. They caused me to learn, pivot (repent), and grow.

My spiritual life was initiated by my family. It was Penne, my wife of forty-three years, who brought me into the Presbyterian Church and surrounded me with an engaged, loving community that turned me in an entirely new direction. The first thirty years, I was a conventional businessman who attended church on a regular basis. I came to church looking for inspiration and served on various committees and the session. Essentially, I was "doing church."

During this season, the faithful messages of three successive senior pastors fanned a small spark in my heart, which began to flicker and grow. But this set up a paradox: the more the flame grew, the less useful to God I felt. A captain in the Salvation Army—who I came to know well—drew my attention to things in my life that needed to change for God to be able to use me. Some of these changes came quickly, others took more time, and others still I continue to face daily. But the grace of God allowed me to enter a new period that I call "being church." I started attending small groups as well as the Sunday worship service which prompted me to share as well as to simply receive.

In the past ten years, my journey has livened up considerably. Through a former pastor, I became aware of Bob Buford, a successful cable-TV businessman who had turned his considerable talents toward enlarging God's kingdom on earth. I flew to Dallas and spent several days with Bob and his associates.

Buford, the founder of the Leadership Network for pastors, had developed a separate ministry for "middle-aged" laypeople who had experienced success but were not completely fulfilled. He called it Halftime, explaining that it was possible to turn the remaining years of our lives into our most significant and joyful years—to finish well.

To go from success to significance meant turning upside down the corporate pyramid that I had climbed for forty years—supporting people instead of people supporting me. Bob and his team, through their resources and personal coaching, created for me a personalized plan that I had not yet been able to formulate on my own.

I returned to the church "all fired up" to be a leader in adult Christian education. But, as we would have expressed it in my jet pilot days, I was "all thrust and no azimuth." While I was comfortable with narrow subjects that I could research, many people come to adult classes with pressing, preloaded questions they feel need answers: Can we rely on the scriptures for guidance today? Is there really a hell? If I am a Catholic, can I receive communion at a Presbyterian church? I felt insufficient in such a role and worried that I would "white knuckle" and offer an off-the-cuff answer that would not be helpful—and may even do harm.

At that point, another divine messenger arrived. Carol Eaton, a fellow elder, listened to my concerns and flatly concluded that I should consider entering seminary. As a seminary graduate herself, she knew the value of submitting your beliefs to the dialectic furnace for refining. So, at the tender age of sixty-four, I entered Fuller Seminary.

You don't go to seminary to find your faith or prove your denominational doctrine. Both of those are sorely tested by people who love Jesus just as much as you do. To maximize dialectic learning, you have to be prepared. The exacting time commitment required for reading, study, and writing soon became apparent to both Penne and me. She remained supportive, proofing some of my papers and even quizzing me with Greek flashcards.

In my third and fourth years of seminary, I began to develop a focus on the issue of faith and wealth. There is much church history and literature on the subject, but it all comes from theologically trained minds. I cannot tell you the number of conversations I have listened to between pastors and session elders about the need to apply better business practices to the running of the church. Others conversely insist that we just need to have a vision, and the money will be there. Despite much confidence supporting each perspective, communication on the matter was difficult because those entering the discussions did not share a common understanding or lexicon. The outcome was often a stunted version of what might have been.

Having a master's degree in economics, I was used to a dispassionate discussion of capital, profit, expenses and other concepts using a common model to make one's point. But not everyone in that conversation was trained in economics—some were trained in the liberal arts and theology.

Theologians have written a copious number of books on the subject of wealth. Secular professors have written an equally copious number of economic books. Depending on which of these perspectives a future leader has ingested, their subsequent teaching and preaching can point to very different life objectives. This dichotomy can bring stress into the life of the believer and does little to ameliorate the pastor–lay leader conversation.

I believed this to be a false dichotomy and that a clearer understanding of biblical teachings could bring integrity into the life of every believer. I realized that I was seeking either an economics textbook written by a theologian or an exegetical Bible commentary on wealth written by a professor of economics. I found neither.

After months of searching and reaching out for recommendations from pastors, faculty, and friends, I located *Foundations of Economics: A Christian View,* by Professor Shawn Ritenour. An economist by training,

Dr. Ritenour teaches at a college committed to a Christian worldview. He is also a proponent of the Austrian School of Economics, which emphasizes that optimal economic outcomes require a free marketplace with minimal outside influence.

I continued to see the need for additional literature that would form a unifying bond between successful business people and pastors. Such a union would accelerate the expansion of God's kingdom on Earth. The Bible provides the basis for that relationship. But it is a rigorous, objective understanding of its teachings, using a common economic model and vocabulary, that seals the bond.

All seminary graduates need to come to grips with their belief on the origin and value of scripture in their lives. All have written papers—and many have written books—to articulate those beliefs. I have offered my own research and beliefs in a sixteen-week course, "How the Scriptures Came to Us." I have taught this course several years now at multiple churches and in various venues. It has strengthened my belief that the Bible is the inspired word of God when read by a similarly inspired reader.

I join with my Scottish ancestors. They were signers of the Solemn League and Covenant of 1643, guided by their faith as expressed in the Westminster Shorter Catechism, which in answer to its first two questions states,

> Man's chief end is to glorify God, and to enjoy him forever.

> The Word of God, which is contained in the Scriptures of the Old and New Testaments, is the only rule to direct us how we may glorify and enjoy him.[1]

I have enjoyed the encouragement of my church community and the Reverend Dr. David Joynt, who offered me a position at Valley Presbyterian Church as scholar in residence so that I might complete this book.

May it be a blessing to you.

May 10, 2017

---

[1] *The Confession of Faith: Together with the Larger and Lesser Catechismes* (London: J. Rothwel, 1658).

PROLOGUE

Let the wise listen and add to their learning,
and let the discerning get guidance—
for understanding proverbs and parables,
the sayings and riddles of the wise.

—Proverbs 1:5–7 (NIV)

At specific times every year, there are huge, joyful gatherings on campuses all across the United States. Friends and family come together to celebrate and witness the largest pay raise that many of the parents sitting in the audience will ever experience.

Jan and Jerry are watching their third and final child walk across the stage. They are already dreaming of embarking on the foreign travel that they have denied themselves for so many years.

Martin is at home with a handful of unpaid bills and the realization that he is heading into his third week of unemployment. He has always been the breadwinner for his family and is becoming depressed. He needs to reach out and share his problem—but with whom?

Sharon is on cloud nine. She has just been hired by the fastest growing tech company in the nation. She will be a software engineer and her starting salary was eye-popping, the medical coverage is good, and her excellent incentive package includes stock options. She is on her way now to the BMW dealership, dreaming of starring in a TV advertisement depicting her motoring off with her attractive and equally successful friends.

Anita is sitting in a quiet house shortly after the memorial service for her husband of forty years. Jim always managed the household finances. She recently received notice that she will be receiving a large life insurance payout. She is very concerned about what to do next.

Melvin and Louise have been very blessed in their long life together. They have self-supporting children and dote on their several grandchildren. They are both Christians, and Melvin has been a very successful businessman. They are now considering their estate.

Jan, Jerry, Martin, Sharon, Anita, Melvin, and Louise know each other as members of the same local Presbyterian church. It is an evangelical church, believing that Jesus changes lives and that scripture forms their foundational beliefs.

John is the associate pastor. He graduated from seminary several years ago and loves serving at this church. He is pleased that the senior pastor has scheduled him to give the sermon this Sunday, one of the weeks leading up to stewardship Sunday.

John knows the church has fallen behind in its pledged giving. Session leaders have encouraged the pastors to be direct in the church's stewardship needs. John feels his gifts are primarily spiritual, and he has always been uncomfortable talking about money. He believes that the love of money is the root of all evil, and he has made his choice between mammon and God. That is why he went to seminary instead of business school like his sister.

Like many preachers, John's sermon preparation has a routine, and the first is to settle on an underlying passage in scripture. He wants to find just the right tone for his congregation. He settles on Luke 12:15 (NASB), "And he said to them, 'Beware, and be on your guard against every form of greed, for not even when one has an abundance does his life consist of his possessions.'"

John prays and then throws himself into preparation of his sermon.

Will John's sermon be helpful to Jan, Jerry, Martin, Sharon, Anita, Melvin, Louise, and the rest of his congregation? Former pastor and now professor and author Michael Moore sees the potential for disaster. He has heard too many such sermons based on what he calls "a polished '3-step' formula":

- Step 1—Shallow overview of selected proof text about wealth and possessions divorced from their literary-historical contexts;
- Step 2—Selective economic prejudices laid over these proof texts designed to champion the instructor's preconceived bias; finally leading up to:

- Step 3—"Authoritative" religious instruction on "what the Bible says" about wealth and possessions.[2]

The results of such a sermon can lead to a cognitive disconnect with the congregation, setting up a dichotomy of life where certain ethics govern six days of their week but then, on Sunday, a different set of principles applies. This can make members feel that they can't take Jesus to the office with them; He has to wait for them at church.

This same cognitive disconnect plays out in church committees across the nation as lay leaders and pastors discuss congregational financial planning and budgeting. Business practices are juxtaposed to faith in God as separate strategies for moving forward.

Does the Bible require such a conflict in the everyday life of the practicing Christian? I do not believe so, if we read and understand the Bible in the language and times that it was written and explain it within a contemporary economic paradigm. The Bible's teachings always provide integrity for the practicing Christian every single day of his or her life.

I first discovered the importance of an economic paradigm while teaching economics at the University of Phoenix. As part of an eclectic career, I had the opportunity to teach middle managers the subjects of Managerial Economics and Corporate Finance. Those students were an ambitious, talented group with strong opinions from their personal, real-world observations. The discussions tended to be loud and cacophonous as they argued based on their individual anecdotal experiences.

But, once some traditional economic paradigms were explained to them, they could quickly relate their experiences in terms of a model. It offered a way to organize their thinking and choose words that would communicate the same meaning to all participants. The discussions became much more productive, and they felt they had a methodology to approach new economic issues when they returned to their respective workplaces.

The value of an economic model goes beyond its ability to contribute to theory and the relationships of certain variables. The ability to add specific numbers in place of the variables generates outcomes that are both predictive and useful in planning and modifying real behavior. Each of the hypothetical people in the prologue can better grasp their financial situation by adding

---

[2] Michael S. Moore, *Wealthwatch: A Study of Socioeconomic Conflict in the Bible* (Eugene: Pickwick Publications, 2011).

their unique numbers and assumptions into the human function $f(h)$, which will be explained later. It will allow them to plan and orient their behavior accordingly. It will help them aim toward **surplus** in their lives and manage it for the glory of God. It will fill their life with abundance, as they know they are living in accordance with God's personal plan for them. The epilogue will reveal some possible outcomes.

The purpose of this book is to introduce some economic paradigms to help explain why God has always required **surplus** for his plan. Further it develops how **surplus** was initiated by God but is perpetuated through humankind. It explains scriptural teachings on how to create **surplus** and why some are given enormous gifts to create **surplus** in order to further His plan. It points out the risk to those that create great **surplus** and the symptoms of soul corrosion that tend to manifest. It concludes that while **surplus** is mandated, only healthy souls who manage or influence that **surplus** are called to be part of His plan of kingdom building.

As important as providing an economic exemplar for a conceptual framework, it is equally important to clearly understand the meaning of the economic teachings of the Bible. To do this, we enter the world of theology and its disciplines. Theological scholars put on virtual-reality goggles to view the world at the time of the writing of the scriptures; virtual earphones allow them to listen to what the writers had to say in their native tongue. This exercise is called "exegesis," where original context meets original communication. Only then are we in a position to apply the stipulated vocabulary of the economic paradigm to the explanation of the teachings, thereby arriving at a systematic overview using authentic biblical motifs or themes. Achieving this goal will provide integrity to the discussion of economics in the Bible so as to avoid any cognitive dissonance between pastors and the business community.

In their preaching, pastors rely to some extent on the commentary and exegesis of others. Such books and commentaries are written by theologians. Professor James A. Metzger has an enviable background in theology, achieving degrees from some of the most prestigious universities. He is a professor of Koine (biblical) Greek and eminently qualified to exegete the Bible. His book *Consumption and Wealth in Luke's Travel Narrative* employs reader-response criticism, narratology (criticism that deals with the structure and function of narrative and its themes, conventions, and symbols) and intertextuality (the relationship between texts) to defend a radical reading of the Gospel's wealth and possessions tradition. He delimits himself to a theological conundrum which came to a head in medieval times but can be traced even earlier. *How does a disciple of Jesus Christ achieve salvation with respect to wealth?* Does he divest himself, or does he give alms? Metzger summarizes, "For disciples, there is simply no middle ground, and Jesus strongly urges them to demonstrate their loyalty to God as well as their commitment to their neighbor through an act of complete divestiture."[3] While at one end of the spectrum, Professor Metzger articulates for many. He is not alone in his thesis. This is one of the positions articulated to all seminary students.

Lay people would not necessarily come into contact with this book—it is written for students and practitioners of theology. But if they did read the book, they would encounter his acknowledgments:

> I am especially appreciative of four years of financial assistance from the United Church of Christ. The "Make a Different Doctoral Study Award" (2002–2006) provided resources each fall to help cover student fees, living expenses, and books for comprehensive exams and dissertation research.

For the people who sit in the pews, this is a cognitive disconnect. How can you, on the one hand, tell people Jesus wants them to divest all of their wealth and then thank, ostensibly the same people, for accumulating and managing wealth to fund your scholarship? This "milk comes from bottles" or "money grows on trees" syndrome cries out for some economic education. Is a wealthy Christian a true oxymoron? Have true disciples of Christ who have created great **surplus** chosen a lesser path that condemns them to regret?

What if there is no gulf between the real world and God's Word on salvation and wealth? What if we don't allow emotion and legacy language to creep into words, such as "wealth" and "mammon"? What if pastors had access to a systematic understanding of the Bible's teachings? What if they could provide guidance that was understandable by those in the workplace today? They would need a resource that bridged the understanding of both parties on the subjects of economics and the Bible.

This book falls within a genre that is called "bridge literature." It harmonizes important thoughts and contributions of two distinct disciplines— theology and economics. It will be read by many people who are trained in one of the disciplines but unfamiliar with the other. While there is a small

---

[3] James A. Metzger, *Consumption and Wealth in Luke's Travel Narrative*, Biblical Interpretation Series (Leiden: Brill, 2007), 132.

group of people with advanced degrees in both subjects, the goal of this book is not to make pastors into accountants, nor businessmen into theologians. Necessarily, we will have to use a lexicon from each discipline to portray our point accurately. But it will not require significant depth. We will not require an understanding of the shortcomings of monophysitism by the accountant; nor will we insist that the pastor grasp the implications of FIFO versus LIFO on EBITDA in an economy of rising prices. If you understood one of those propositions, this book is meant to be helpful to you. However, the reader may encounter words that are new to them. We will try not to interrupt the book's reading by employing parallel explanation and footnotes where warranted. But it should not be surprising if the reader encounters some unfamiliar vocabulary or concepts that need to be acquired.

We must increase our comprehension of the alternative body of knowledge by a certain amount if we are to find mutual understanding. One hoped-for outcome of this book is to build shared comprehension in the body of Christ. Approaching such a goal will be indicated if the reader appreciates the body of knowledge and its expression that is brought by the other party.

The thesis of this book is that the economics of God is systematic and that His economic plan mandates **surplus**. In support of that mandate, certain people have been and are given special gifts and called to be leading actors in creating **surplus**. That call is second to no other call that God issues. All of God's calls are for His purpose. The call issued to highly productive people is to employ their special gifts in order to maximize **surplus** and deploy it for His purposes. Optimal situations can occur when theological leaders with great vision are yoked to great **surplus** creators through a common understanding of God's teachings and plan. Their mutual support for each other's spiritual health and effective plan execution has in the past and will in the future create great outcomes with God's blessing. May this book be a vehicle toward fostering more such *koinonia*, or Christian cooperative ventures.

1

HASN'T THE CHURCH TALKED ABOUT THIS BEFORE?

For it is easier for a camel to go through the eye of a needle
than for a rich man to enter the kingdom of God.

—Matthew 19:24 (NASB)

Wealth and money have been subjects of church teaching from the beginning. That is because they are frequent subjects of the Bible. But the commentary has been verse by verse and parable by parable. In this book, we will discuss the lack of systematic models and the concomitant confusion that have encased the subjects for years.

The chorus of leading church voices on the subject of wealth and money does not create harmony. There are many soloists who seem to make sense when heard individually, but their voices become confusing when heard together. It can leave us conflicted and confused when we hear powerful theologians and pastors such as John Calvin say,

He furnished the world with all things needful, and even with an immense profusion of wealth, before he formed man. Thus, man was rich before he was born.[4]

If you have been assigned the goods of this world by God and don't share them with others, it isn't just stinginess, it is injustice.[5]

The Bible makes it clear that it's just plain foolishness not to manage your money well. And foolishness never ends well. Proverbs 21:20 says, "Wise people live in wealth and luxury, but stupid people spend their money as fast as they get it" (GNT).[6]

Those who worship money increasingly define themselves in terms of it and increasingly treat other people as creditors, debtors, partners, or customers rather than as human beings.[7]

These voices seem to provide diverse understandings of how disciples of Jesus are to work, support their families, and provide for their retirement in the world today. If these theologians had access to a helpful economic model and a defined economic lexicon, they might find that their voices were in better harmony than it would appear.

The well-respected contributors to the *Dictionary: New Testament Background*, who are fair in their tolerance and inclusive in points of view, conclude, "Jesus followers are still left perhaps with uneasy consciences in times that celebrate mammon and the successes of industrial and technological capitalism."[8]

---

[4] Steven Wedgeworth, "John Calvin on the Use of Goods and Money," The Calvinist International, www.calvinistinternational.com, accessed 2017.

[5] Holly Marr, "11 Inspiring Quotes from Tim Keller," *Logos Talk* (Logos Bible Software, 2016).

[6] Rick Warren, "Use This Simple Principle to Manage Your Money Well," *Pastor Rick's Daily Hope* (2015).

[7] Keith Ferrin, "We Become What We Worship—Nt Wright," *Keith Ferrin Blog*, accessed 2017.

[8] Craig A. Evans and Stanley E. Porter, *Dictionary of New Testament Background* (Downers Grove: InterVarsity Press, 2000), 909.

While an "uneasy conscience" was often precipitated by the radical teachings of Jesus in his time, it was not where he wanted his followers to remain. He wanted them to understand and embrace his teachings so they could propagate them with a clear and confident voice. He taught in parables so that his message could be grasped more quickly and repeated accurately. These goals are similar to the scientific models used today, with their defined terminology.

Many pastors feel they can dodge and weave successfully through an obstacle course of cacophonous communications on wealth and arrive spiritually intact. They typically explain how they do so in an idiosyncratic manner that does not always resonate in the experience of their hearers. This has not led to a unified stentorian voice from the church on the role of wealth (**surplus**) in God's plan.

Part of the issue is that religious leaders are most often PhDs in philosophy or theology. Rarely do they hold MBAs or advanced economic degrees. Jesus told us in Matthew 4:4, "Man shall not live on bread alone, but on every word that comes from the mouth of God." So, our religious leaders must be people trained in the Word and provide it to us. But that same passage also builds on the premise that bread is food and necessary to survive. The provision of food requires an understanding of economics.

Conversely, more people in business are trained in economics than in theology. Businesses organize and operate using terminology such as *capital*, *costs*, and *market elasticity*. They don't talk much about using the philosophy of Plato's forms or using the Socratic method to derive truth in running their businesses. Their application of theology is generally limited to secularly appropriated aphorisms such as the Golden Rule.

How did this chasm between theology and business develop? Is it as wide and unbridgeable as many today profess? Or is it a false dichotomy maintained by those who do not have a Christian worldview? Can a better understanding of biblical teachings and a modern economic explanation bring integrity to God's plan and our everyday lives? These important questions cannot be addressed without an understanding of how the break began in the first place. It did not happen all at once. It happened over an extended period, driven by motivations that many have forgotten.

Many people who have generated **surplus** have used a background in economics, accounting, or business administration to great effect. It is important for them to know that using those tools is not contrary to the Bible. A brief review may help.

2
A SPLIT, THEN A CREVASSE, AND FINALLY A CHASM

Such people do not comprehend and cannot understand,
for he has shut their eyes so they cannot see,
and their minds so they cannot understand.

—Isaiah 44:18 (CSB)

In this chapter, we will look at the evolution of understanding about the natural sciences that, unfortunately, created a dichotomy of thinking for some—the idea that the Bible and science are in conflict with each other. To better understand this, we must retrace eight hundred years of human critical analysis.

In the thirteenth century, Thomas Aquinas, a great church theologian and philosopher, summarized principles of scholasticism that harmonized biblical teachings with the practices of everyday life. They demonstrated that people could be confident in the church's ability to give guidance for their everyday activities. The principles were considered informative of nature. This study of the world as experienced was called natural philosophy. To maintain their authority as theologians, the church extrapolated the Bible into areas that were not intended. Over time, their explanations for the relationship between heavenly bodies and the form of the earth were replaced. Empirical observation provided better bases for describing a solar system and the earth as an orb. Some in the church resisted bitterly and forced a split to begin.

Most historians hold that natural philosophy, as a whole, was replaced by modern science over a span of years called the Enlightenment (1685–1815). The Enlightenment was an ebullient period in which humanity fell in love with its ability to reason. Reason provided rapid improvements in the quality of life. It proved an effective weapon against all forms of institutional tyranny—both secular and religious. And it insisted on individual accountability for morals and ethics. The split became a crevasse.

Two of its leading lights, Isaac Newton and Adam Smith, are pertinent to this book. Later commentators would say that the written works of these two men would point to a chasm between the Bible and economics, a chasm so wide that it could never be bridged. But those are the conclusions of subsequent observers and not of Newton and Smith themselves.

Newton was brought up as an Anglican. Smith was raised as a Presbyterian. Great Britain was experiencing multidimensional power struggles among Anglicans, Presbyterians, Episcopalians, other Protestants sects, and Catholics. Both men were skeptics of organized religion—particularly the Roman Catholic Church. But both men were personally committed to God and immersed themselves in voluminous writings on the nature of God and the morality of humans. They were not atheists. Their mutual interest was to remove the influence of church hierarchies over everyday lives, not to replace God with reason.

Newton wrote the *Philosophiae Naturalis Principia Mathematica* (1687), providing mathematical proofs (using his new study of infinitesimals) to prove empirical observations. His study of infinitesimals along with that of his contemporary, Gottfried Leibniz, have become known as calculus, a powerful method of expressing and solving complex mathematical functions. But Newton was also a biblical exegete. He wrote *An Historical Account of Two Notable Corruptions of Scripture* in 1690 against the Catholic Church as proof that it was supporting Trinitarianism by consciously modifying scripture. And yet, he would praise Luther and Erasmus for having scriptural integrity. Newton would become a Unitarian.

Adam Smith wrote the *Inquiry into the Nature and Causes of the Wealth of Nations* in 1776. It contained a description of a free market for goods that established price through the selfish interest of its participants. This study of markets and the effects of changes in supply and demand have caused many economic historians to demarcate its publishing as the beginning of the science of economics. But before he wrote on economics, Smith wrote a treatise explaining the actions of humans based on their nature and motivation for happiness. The book was entitled *The Theory of Moral Sentiments* and was published in 1741. In it, his economic man was also a moral man. And while that man was guided between the competing forces of passion and empathy, his morality was weighed in the context of God's ultimate judgment. Smith also describes the unobservable force that brings equilibrium to the marketplace as an "invisible hand." He acknowledges that humans act within a framework constructed by God. He concludes, "The care of the universal happiness of all rational and sensible beings, is the business of God and not of man." Smith would become an Episcopalian.

Four centuries after the Enlightenment, Christians continue to enjoy the improvements in their quality of life that science provides. While supporting science, they still feel the purpose and fulfillment of life is best addressed by the Bible. Evangelists believe that the Bible as stated in 2 Timothy 3:16 "is God-breathed and is useful for teaching, rebuking, correcting and training in righteousness." This includes every aspect of our everyday lives, including our time at work and being productive. They feel that science and empiricism demonstrate the grand complexity and greatness of the creation bringing greater appreciation and glory to God.

The language of science better describes the world we physically live in today. The Bible used a more limited vocabulary and fewer empirical observations to explain its great truths to its original hearers. One objective of this book is to develop the Bible's motifs using a modern scientific lexicon in such a way that the everyday business person of today sees the truth of its guidance as well. Thanks to Adam Smith and Isaac Newton, we can communicate using economic models. They are able to show the relationship of variables in order to inform predictive behavior. We can thank Isaac Newton for the fact that the models can provide discrete answers using calculus for complex functions. Interweaving the lessons of scripture with economic models demonstrates their applicability not only for predictive behavior but more importantly for normative behavior that agrees with God's plan.

This bridge over the chasm allows us to now move forward to see what God has revealed about his economic plan and to explain those revelations using contemporary economic models. We will also be able enter personal numerical assumptions in the model to provide mathematical answers which will help guide our own personal actions.

We believe people who build **surplus** using economics can maintain their belief in God and his sovereignty over the earth and their lives. Adam Smith and Isaac Newton did.

3

EXEGETICAL ECONOMICS—
THE BRIDGE

The heart of the discerning acquires knowledge,
for the ears of the wise seek it out.

—Proverbs 18:15 (NIV)

One of the retardants of ecumenical thinking about economics and the Bible is that those professionally trained in only one of those subjects use words that look and sound alike but have different meanings and nuances. In this chapter, we will examine the challenge in coming to common understandings and common ground.

Some say the chasm perceived between the science of economics and the theological understanding of the Bible cannot be bridged. This is because the concepts of profit and wealth are valued very differently by those trained in theology from those trained in economics. Insular training over the years has only served to harden the disparate positions and make communication more difficult. We shall explain.

A pastor, economist, and businessman enter a meeting room to find common ground on the management of their church. Each is an experienced professional and strongly convicted in his or her views. The pastor has a foundational belief in scripture and is convinced that mammon is the root of all evil. The economist has several advanced degrees in his field and is convinced that reasonable assumptions make for a useful model to demonstrate how a profit is derived. The businessman can't wait to "tell it like it is" in the "real world," where he has managed to become wealthy. Such a meeting will likely generate more heat than light.

Many of us probably fit into one of these categories. In preparing for such a meeting, we should not begin by reviewing our own approach. We should start by reviewing the mindset of the other participants. This requires learning their structure and vocabulary. To start with, let's look at various ways of legitimately talking about economics.

THE WORD, THE SUBJECT, AND THE THEORY

A discussion on any topic requires agreement on the subject matter. When someone announces he is talking about economics, does it mean that he is discussing the word, the subject, or a theory? This may be confusing to those who are accustomed to entering the discussion of economics at an assumed entry point.

The complication is that we don't all enter the discussion at the *same* entry point. Theologians, professors, and practitioners all enter the study of economics at different points. They necessarily orient their students to their own starting point in order to build from their own perspective. Let us compare these different perspectives not only for what they can teach us about another's perspective but also to appreciate that an ecumenical conversation on economics must contain a preamble.

THE WORD

Theologians primarily begin their study of economics with the word and its etymology. That is because seminary is focused in a major way on understanding scripture. A number of courses train and refine the future pastor's or theologian's ability to individually analyze the meaning of passages of scripture in the context that they were written. This is called exegetics.

Their conclusions are explained in contemporary language using examples and applications in everyday living for better lay comprehension. This is called hermeneutics. These are, in fact, some of the most important pastoral duties. So, they study the original scriptural languages of Hebrew and Koine Greek. Consequently, they are not limited to the interpretation of third party translators regarding the meaning or idea contained in the verse.

Just as importantly, they are trained to spot the most significant word in the verse for special consideration and study. Appropriately, this is called a "word study." So, pastors and theologians can begin a discussion of the topic of economics on grounds unfamiliar and unplowed by most secular economic scholars and practitioners. Because they want to learn what God has to say about economics, they begin with the word οἰκονομία (oikonomia: management of household affairs) which most dictionaries provide as the root word for "economics."

Οἰκονομία is a compound word made up of the words οἶκος (*oikos*, meaning house or household) and νόμος (*nomos*, meaning law) and thereby coming up with the literal definition of "rules of the household." Like most words, it will take on cultural assumptions and come to mean more than one thing. BDAG, the primary Greek-English scriptural lexicon, provides three prime meanings of οἰκονομία with additional subprime nuances.[9] It has been used to mean "responsibility of management," "state of being arranged," and "program of instruction."

The other crucial discipline applied in a word study is context. The investigator must stop the time-travel elevator at the right floor of history, get out, and look around. Those that do that regarding the context of οἰκονομία will immerse themselves in the early centuries of the Roman Empire and its influence on subject nations, such the Judean Kingdom of Israel.

Most find a major implication in the Roman law of *Patria potestas* (Latin: "power of a father"), which granted legal status to the absolute power of the eldest male member of the family over all other members and extended household of the family. This was compatible with the patriarchal social structure of the tribes in the nation of Israel. It should be noted, however, that the different moral beliefs of the Jewish and Roman fathers resulted in very different decisions.

Some secular scholars and theologians will find common ground in engaging Aristotle's use of οἰκονομία and his contribution to the meaning of the term some four hundred years earlier. Aristotle wrote broadly on flows of value, money and its use, and a system beyond the household to include various forms of polity. But he applied the term itself only to the natural and ethical ways of value creation from labor and the land. He alternatively used

---

[9] Walter Bauer, *A Greek-English Lexicon of the New Testament and Other Early Christian Literature*, ed. Frederick William Danker, trans. F. Wilbur Gingrich and William F. Arndt, 3rd ed. (Chicago: The University of Chicago Press, 1957), 697.

the term χρηματιστική (*chrematisticae*: commerce) to talk about the art of getting rich from trading and exchange, which he frowned upon ethically.

We can conclude that participants in the discussion of economics would overwhelmingly agree that the etymology of the word lies in its Greek origins. Many theologians will see a confluence of biblical and Aristotelian thinking on wealth and conclude that they need not investigate economics any further—wealth is both unethical and sinful. A broader understanding of economics, then, is not necessary. This is not helpful for their congregations. Secular scholars will say that while Aristotle distinguished between οἰκονομία and χρηματιστική on an ethical basis, the subjects are intertwined and not *de facto* pejorative.[10]

Further, economists will contend that none of the Greek writings provide for a systematic understanding of commerce today. They argue we must wait centuries for the subject of political economy to develop. Such conclusions simply reinforce the idea of a chasm.

THE SUBJECT

The subject of economics has retrospectively connected itself to the original human need for basic survival. The subject itself took on additional forms and substance as societies organized for their collective survival. The earliest forms of economic formation were top-down and authoritarian in nature, reflecting the political and religious power structures of the time. Whether the authority came from military power or divine revelation, the system collected food, concentrated its holdings, and distributed food back to the populace for political and religious purposes.

Some have called this a "command" economic system; others have called it a "distributive" economic system.[11] The body of economic writing at the time was assembled for the purpose of observation and assessing the ethical nature of the intransigent *status quo*. Studying that body of knowledge was not expected to change one's standard of living. Only through inheritance or capturing the assets of a vanquished foe could one experience riches in a single

---

[10] Robert L. Heilbroner, *Teachings from the Worldly Philosophy* (New York: W.W. Norton, 1996), 6–10.

[11] Jacob Neusner, *The Economics of the Mishnah* (Chicago: University of Chicago Press, 1990).

lifetime. Trusted advisors and stewards had a limited ability to build wealth through service to the powerful, thus, effectively reinforcing their hegemony.

But there came a time when it was recognized that peace was actually the best prerequisite for individual and national wealth accumulation. Such an atmosphere of security allowed for a dramatic broadening of exchange, morphing society's commerce into a marketplace economy. Requisite changes in land ownership, political formation, rights of citizens, religious perspectives, scientific advancements, artisan developments, and other factors would take a millennium to develop. This intriguing evolution—and sometimes revolution—of human cooperation to better survive is well beyond the scope of our needs here. By the eighteenth century, the description of what was going on in everyday commerce was fathomable to the ordinary participant. But it was too large, too diverse, and too complex for coherent government policy.

Then some great minds made individual contributions that, together, gave the body of economic knowledge more structure. Adam Smith opined that it was the self-interest of individuals acting on their own behalf that created a self-regulating market, as if governed by an "invisible hand," and to "thus without intending it, without knowing it, advance the interest of the society, and afford means to the multiplication of the species."[12] Some other contributors, including Thomas Malthus, Jeremy Bentham, and Frédéric Bastiat, introduced such issues as human sustainability, pursuit of happiness, and free trade into economic discourse. But it was Isaac Newton's *Philosophiæ Naturalis Principia Mathematica* that explained the calculus of infinitesimals that allowed economists to explain the relationship of variables in nonlinear graphical form. Thus, a formal body of knowledge called by the explicit name of economics was recognized.

Those that studied the subject became known as economists and advanced their understanding through pure reason. And because the relationships between variables was demonstrable using the latest mathematical developments, it became known as a science as opposed to philosophy. Reason as guided by science was now going to guide human destiny. Economics, like the other sciences, was viewed as the new lodestone taking humanity forward without regard to traditional sources of wisdom such as the Bible and the church. Christians were now faced with a dichotomy. Learn economics to

---

[12] Adam Smith, *An Inquiry into the Nature and Causes of the Wealth of Nations*, 5th ed., 3 vols. (London: A. Strahan, 1789), 540.

succeed in this world and study the Bible for salvation in the next. Theology lost its relevance to even join in the discussion of how to contribute to the improvement of the macro human condition in the modern world.

But has that worked? Postmodernists question reliance on reason as the sole arbiter of the human condition. As S. J. Barnett notes, "They argue … that the modern project was a costly failure, bringing not the sweet dreams of reason, but war, famine, disease and ecological disaster."[13]

With both economists and theologians equally threatened with irrelevance or censure, maybe the preconditions for a meaningful dialogue require a closer look at how the world really works—the businessman's point of view. To explore that possibility, we must develop a theory that closely reflects our observations in the real world.

THE THEORY

Seeking truth is the mutual goal of the theologian and the economist—truth that is reflected in the real world of our existence. Theologians believe God provides our understanding of that truth. They therefore seek God's truth through the general revelation of the Creation and the special revelation of scripture.

The economist seeks truth through reason by proposing theories of human interaction based on crucial assumptions. The majority of economists build on classical economics and feel that as more and more data can be collected and applied, the more relevant will be their theories. This has led to specialized economic subjects such as cost-benefit analysis, econometrics, and game theory. However, even as vast amounts of data have been crunched by ever-more-powerful computers, some economists see problems.

Beginning in the 1970s—about the same time as the postmodern movement—behavioral economics began to question the math-driven models of classical and Keynesian theories. It pointed out that, while the models proved mathematically the relationship between certain variables, they were not reflective of the real world. The problem was that their assumed, static, rational human being was not present in the real world. Thus, their assumptions made them GIGO (garbage in, garbage out)—in the parlance of computer science.

---

[13] S. J. Barnett, *The Enlightenment and Religion: The Myths of Modernity* (Manchester: Manchester University Press, 2003).

Behavioral economics, on the other hand, would "be done with strong injections of good psychology and other social sciences."[14] Such economists feel that a more enriched economic science is necessary to reflect the real world. However, it is the businessman who practices economics every day who must validate such a model by using it for making everyday decisions. Such a behavioral model has not yet presented itself.

In pursuit of such a model, another economic school of thought has been regaining momentum. It is termed the Austrian School and applies what is called the praxeology method. The original threads of the school were identified by the fifteenth-century theologian Thomas Aquinas. He and his scholastic followers "discovered and explained the laws of supply and demand, the cause of inflation, the operation of foreign exchange rates, and the subjective nature of economic value."[15] That thread continued diachronically through a number of economists, such as Claude Frédéric Bastiat, who maintained the same premise while influenced by the work of Adam Smith and others. In 1871, Carl Menger incorporated, expanded, and organized the previous threads into economic principles that founded the Austrian School of Economics.

Unlike behavioral economists, who seek positivism through studies of the human brain, Menger builds his foundation on the human being as a whole as they interpret subjective value and determine diminishing marginal utility. There is a covalence of thinking between Menger and theologians who believe that the entire holistic human body, made in the image of God, is the minimum required organic complexity necessary to observe true human social interaction. Professor Shawn Ritenour has embraced this covalent thinking, as he explains,

> The approach that is the most realistic and meaningful method of discovering economics is verbal logical deduction. Beginning with the axiom that *humans act,* we can use verbal statements to logically deduce principles of economics that—as long as we do not make any mistakes in our logic—are themselves true. True not just at one point in time, but true

---

[14] Richard H. Thaler, *Misbehaving: The Making of Behavioral Economics* (New York: W. W. Norton & Company).

[15] "Misesinstitute Austrian Economics, Freedom, and Peace." https://mises.org/about-mises/what-austrian-economics.

for all time. This method has been called the praxeological method (praxeology meaning the study of human action) and is the method most identified with the Austrian School of economics.[16]

Professor Ritenour has written a comprehensive textbook on economics in the tradition of the Austrian School. Further, he frequently explains the compatibility of his models with scripture providing a Christian view of existential economics in the world today. He joins a number of economic professors across the nation that feel there is compatibility between the scriptures and how the world works as described through an economic lens.

But there is a great difference between using contemporary biblical commentary and scriptural quotes to support economic models *ex post facto* and using economic models to better understand scriptural teachings and interpretations *a priori*. I believe economics as a discipline can provide for a better understanding of the scripture in the first place. Communicating those teachings in a singular consistent mode will result in better comprehension, better choices, and a much more fulfilled life for the Christian working in the secular marketplace. This approach is a novel application of economics and deserves a special designation.

EXEGETICAL ECONOMICS

I believe there is a vast opportunity to use established economic models to extract and explain the economic truths of the Bible. Such models provide the ability to dialogue with mutual professional respect regarding differences without the vague, sometimes-emotive legacy language otherwise employed. Much like how neurosurgeons calmly debate the way to proceed in a life-critical operating situation while loved ones pray and cry in the waiting room, we must find a way to have respectful dialogue without diatribe to achieve the best outcomes.

The use of economic models to demonstrate the truths of the Bible extracted with traditional exegetical tools, I term "exegetical economics." Its development is aimed at enhancing communication, harmony, and progress in building God's Kingdom on Earth.

---

[16] Shawn Ritenour, *Foundations of Economics: A Christian View* (Eugene: Wipf and Stock Publishers, 2010), 18.

In the following chapters, we will propose a couple of applications of economic models to communicate Biblical truths concerning the creation and **surplus** generation. Those truths should be employed in our lives today. But these models are just the beginning. There is vast opportunity to employ additional economic models regarding biblical teaching on the environment, the economic social fabric, organizational charters, etc.

4
APPLYING ECONOMICS TO THE BIBLE

So he called him in and asked him,
"What is this I hear about you?
Give an account of your management,
because you cannot be manager any longer."

—Luke 16:2 (NIV)

This chapter will look at why economics is an appropriate tool to better understand the Bible, and it will propose some helpful economic models.

Economics, like all the sciences, is a construct of the human mind, that marvelous mind that was created by God. And while the mind has vastly improved our living experience here on Earth, it is lesser than the Mind that rules eternity. Consequently, we must approach the scriptures, which are the revelation of the greater Mind, humbly but deliberately. After all, there are things he wants us to understand. He wishes us wisdom and an abundant life. Like medicine, physics, and psychology, let us apply economics in that endeavor.

Economics has become the discipline that quantifies choices from which business people make decisions. These decisions fundamentally determine how we interact with each other. Business uses the materials of the creation in generating their products. Those decisions are also quantified according to the discipline of economics. Here is how several colleges describe the value of an economic background in today's world:

Economics is about choice and the impact of our choices on each other. It relates to every aspect of our lives, from the decisions we make as individuals or families to the structures created by governments and firms. The economic way of thinking can help us make better choices.[17]

Studying economics includes learning to use statistics and to read critically. Economics majors are interesting people both because of their skills and because they can explain why economic phenomena occur and how economic performance might improve.[18]

Many, if not most, of the nation's and the world's most significant social problems have an economic dimension. ... The study of economics is an excellent way to acquire problem-solving skills and develop a logical, ordered way of looking at problems. It leads naturally to careers in business, law, and in economics research and consulting.[19]

It would seem that using economic language to describe God's guidance for our lives might prove useful to such people.

"God's peace means that in God's being and in His actions, He is separate from all confusion and disorder."[20] In other words, he is systematic, and I believe that extends to his economics. Under our heading of *exegetical economics,* the first theory might be very broad and designated a general theory. Consequently, we define the general economic theory of the Bible as the interaction of humankind with the creation and each other for the purpose of growing and flourishing according to God's plan. Using the tools of the exegete—original languages and ancient context—we can see repeated biblical motifs that lend themselves to such a systematic understanding.

---

[17] "Why Study? Economics," The University of Bristol, http://whystudyeconomics. ac.uk/, accessed 2017.

[18] Rupi Saggi, "Why Study Economics?" Vanderbilt College of Arts and Science, https:// as.vanderbilt.edu/econ/undergraduate/why-study-economics.php, accessed 2017 2017.

[19] "Why Study Economics?" Washington University in St. Louis https://economics. wustl.edu/undergraduate/whyecon, accessed 2017.

[20] Wayne A. Grudem, *Systematic Theology: An Introduction to Biblical Doctrine* (Grand Rapids: Inter-Varsity Press, 1994), 203.

Within this large model, there is a discrete model relating to human economic actions within the creation. That subset model I term the human function $f(h)$. We will be dealing with both models, the human function $f(h)$ and the creation model C within which the human function operates.

From a Christian perspective, there is more to humankind than their physical existence here on earth. Created in the image of God, humans have spiritual dimensions that cannot be easily quantified. So, we delimit our models to capture only those human actions that we can quantify by our five earthly senses. Each person will reflect his or her own unique values for the parameters contained in the human function $f(h)$. The model will demonstrate that while the amount of focus and interest in each variable may differ from person to person, the relationship of the variables to each other remains constant.

THE GENERAL ECONOMIC THEORY OF THE BIBLE

We first turn to the all-subsuming general economic theory of the Bible. It is impossible for humans to state it in its entirety. It is simply too complex and dynamic. But we have made some tantalizing discoveries of what it must include. It must include the law of conservation of mass, which states that matter is neither created nor destroyed formulated by Antoine Lavoisier in 1785. With that in mind, a Christian will come to the following conclusions: first, the fact that the creation exists calls for a God who can create something from nothing, or *ex nihilo*, and second, the amount of mass at the time of the Garden of Eden is equal to the amount of mass today, even though the world looks substantially different. Much of that difference is due to humans who have grown in substantial numbers.

Another tantalizing fact is that scientists have identified a number of precise conditions necessary to maintain expanding life in the creation including water, temperature, gases, and solar radiation—all in precise amounts. The precision and tolerances of these variables is so tight that any departure from them would end life on Earth. Scientists have not been able to find these same variables in the same precise tolerances anywhere else in the universe. Christian scientists call this phenomenon the "fine-tuning of the universe" and another factor pointing toward a creator God. Stanford's online *Encyclopedia of Philosophy* has numerous articles around the subject.

Some rudimentary models, but very sophisticated in human terms, can be built around the actions of the troposphere. Just think of the hurricane tracking models that NOAA (National Oceanic and Atmospheric Administration) uses to predict the tracks of hurricanes each year. When they first identify the disturbance, it is out in the Atlantic and they show five or six possible tracks of the storm. Some show it going back out to sea, some show it going up the East Coast, and some show it proceeding along the Gulf Coast. The different tracks are models that contain different assumptions, variables, and coefficients. Despite the urgency in saving lives and property, meteorologists have not been able to specify a single correct model. It isn't until the storm moves closer to land that the models agree more and more. There are fewer variables.

Humans will forge ahead with such models that are predictive and improve our life experience. However, we should not anticipate that humankind will develop the infinitely more complex function C for the creation as a whole.

The difference between other planets, moons, and asteroids that are just cold hard rocks and the earth is the earth's ability to sustain life—its vitality. God's plan calls for the sustaining and flourishing of life here on Earth. The creation does this dynamically by constantly reforming its fixed amount of mass. Photosynthesis takes place in plants. Mitosis takes place in cells. Procreation takes place in humans. This ability of the creation to constantly reform its matter in such a way as to sustain life, I call Creation Vitality C_v. The essence of C_v is the ecosystem, which contains inert matter and living organisms, all functioning together to maintain stasis. Humankind is the organism made in the image of God and given the responsibility of stewardship of the ecosystem. This requires active management as humans pursue their own function to grow and flourish. The human function of growth and flourishing is also part of God's plan. Many chemical reactions go into the rejuvenation of the earth each day. But with the current and growing population density of the earth, none are more important than the daily actions of humankind.

C_v, then, is one of the most important parameters contained in the Creation function C. It is revealed to us in the Bible. Inert material is continually being transformed into living flora and fauna. Creation Vitality (C_v) is just as important to life as all of the other fine-tuning tolerances previously mentioned. Biblical teachings demonstrate that humans have been commanded to take care of the creation so as to maintain its C_v. Humans are not to take actions that devastate the flora and fauna of the earth, such as polluting the earth with careless byproducts of their living. C_v must remain above zero if God's plan for humans is to succeed.

19

Because the economics of the Bible is systematic, economic tools can be used to better understand the teachings of the Bible in a number of ways. One of the ways is to use econometrics to better understand our stewardship of the creation, as reinforced in the Noahic covenant and many other teachings. Econometrics uses statistics to relate variables to each other and over time. This is called regression analysis and can be shown as a formula. The Creation viability formula might be expressed as $C_v = \beta_0 + \beta_1 f(h) + G_t$, where C_v is the dependent variable expressing the ability of the creation to rejuvenate itself, β_0 is the value of that vitality on day 6 of creation, β_1 is the slope of the C_v function, $f(h)$ is the independent variable expressing the human function (production-consumption), and G_t is God's purposed intervention in the creation. The star is merely an enhanced, divinely caused data point. The graph might appear as follows:

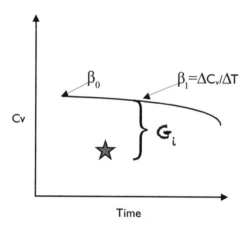

There are a number of nuances to the creation vitality function as opposed to other linear regressions. This function is unique with regard to time. While the function begins on God's day zero, β_0 doesn't actually intercept the y-axis since the creation was not vital until day 6. The slope of the function is inferred to be negative due to the independent variable $f(h)$, representing the human function. We empirically know that byproducts of the human function such as plastic waste and carbon dioxide interfere and diminish C_v. Humanity's exponential growth has put ever greater pressure on C_v due to farming, ranching, and fishing. Producing the energy required to be more productive has caused associated accidents, such as Chernobyl and the *Exxon Valdez*, putting additional significant pressure on the environment. So not only is β_1 negative, but it is turning more so as the velocity of the human function increases with population growth. Finally, G_i would represent data points that are a departure from C_v that are caused by the human function alone. Those would include ice ages, warming periods, storms, volcanic action, and other phenomena which insurers term "acts of God." Christians believe that God has interdicted history on multiple occasions to affect human vitality, both negatively and positively, as in the cases of the Great Flood, Sodom and Gomorrah, the provision of manna and water to the Exodus Israelites, or the causing of heavenly bodies to be stationary, such as in Joshua 10:12. His intercessions, by definition, are purposed. This model does not resolve the debate that current deleterious effects on the creation, such as global warming, are primarily caused by God or humankind.

$f(h)$, as represented in the equation, represents God's mandate for humankind to multiply and flourish. He created an urge for union that would result in progeny (Gen. 3:16). Later, he blessed Noah and his sons repeatedly saying, "Be fertile and increase, and fill the earth" (Gen. 9:1, 7). God's blessing is different from God's intervention. God's blessing is conveyed so that a human endeavor may be good and pleasing as described in Romans 12:2. God's intervention, as used in the model, is a solo interdiction at different times in human history to change its trajectory.

God's blessing is typified in his covenant with Abraham when he took him outside, saying, "Look toward heaven and count the stars, if you are able to count them." And he added, "So shall your offspring be" (Gen. 15:5). The completion of the covenant was achieved through a faithful human being, not a divine act. Since writing was developed, human history has recorded that the growth and expansion of humanity has occurred at an ever-increasing rate. God's blessing has become an important part of the human function. Greater achievement is accomplished if the human endeavor is consonant with God's plan and intention. Realizing this, many Christians pray for guidance with regard to important economic endeavors or decisions.

Christians do not believe that God created the earth as a ball of cheese to be consumed and finally exhausted by an exponentially growing family of creatures. However, not everyone shares that view. In a recent newspaper article, a very respected scientist, Professor Stephen Hawking, commented, "The human species will have to populate a new planet within 100 years if it is to survive. ... Earth's cataclysmic end may be hastened by humankind, which will continue to devour the planet's resources at unsustainable rates."[21] Hawking sees a dead planet unable to sustain life as our near-term future. It is his scientific eschatology.

Christians do believe in an eschatology, or the ending of history as we know it. It will be driven by God, and its conclusion will attain the goal he set out for creation. It will be a time of assessment, but God will bless those who have clung to their foundational belief in scripture and lived their lives accordingly.[22] But the eschaton and its timing is in God's hands. We are taught neither to be preoccupied with it nor to be the cause of it—simply to anticipate it and be ready.[23]

Epidemics, population growth, or damage to the environment could be a reason to abandon Earth. That is not to say that a flourishing Earth is not part of God's staging plan to populate other parts of His creation in the cosmos. However, it has been known from scriptural times that the creation is subject to stress from sinful humans and awaits its own liberty.[24]

In Moses's time, God provided direct guidance on sustainability which set apart the Jewish nation in their interaction with the land. This instruction from God was included by Moses in the latter part of Leviticus and has been termed part of the "Holiness Code."[25] Specifically within that code, a "Shabbat of the Lord" (a time of complete rest) was to be granted to the land.[26] The land was allowed to be fallow. It was not to be planted or harvested for an entire year in the last year of a seven-year cycle. God knew long before man that the natural return of decayed nutrients to the ground was necessary to maintain its vitality—its ability to support vegetation and therefore humanity. Since that time, humans have learned ways to reintroduce nutrients to the ground more quickly so as not to lose an entire growing season. The result is

---

[21] Peter Holley, "Stephen Hawking Just Moved up Humanity's Deadline for Escaping Earth," *The Washington Post,* https://www.washingtonpost.com/news/speaking-of-science/wp/2017/05/05/stephen-hawking-just-moved-up-humanitys-deadline-for-escaping-earth/?utm_term=.684a61973b43, accessed 2017.

[22] Revelation 22:12–17.

[23] Matthew 24:36–46.

[24] Romans 8:19–22.

[25] Everett Fox, *The Five Books of Moses : Genesis, Exodus, Leviticus, Numbers, Deuteronomy: A New Translation with Introductions, Commentary, and Notes* (New York: Schocken Books, 1995), 223.

[26] Adele Berlin and others, *The Jewish Study Bible* (Oxford: Oxford University Press, 2004), 269.

that a much larger population is being sustained. But that does not mean that all modern approaches such as deforestation are a benefit to the environment globally.

Thus, in our time, those guided by scripture see the need to continue engagement on the sustainability of the creation. As encouraged by Jesus, they are joining with local and regional groups on ecological projects large and small. On a global basis, some religious leaders are bringing together scientists, politicians, and a spectrum of theologians to deal with the issues of an "integral ecology." The Vatican is making a major effort by establishing two Pontifical Academies.

> In May 2014, the two academies of scholars, philosophers and theologians met to contemplate the sustainability of humanity and nature and came to a remarkable (for a scientific body) conclusion: The resolution of major environmental problems facing society requires a fundamental reorientation in our behavior and attitude towards nature and toward each other.[27]

One of the goals of *Exegetical Economics* is to allow Christians to engage and support both such concerns by elucidating them with paradigms and vocabulary that aids communication and understanding.

THE HUMAN FUNCTION F(H)

The human function derives ontologically from its relationship to food and water. That relationship is explained in numerous places in the Bible. The human function f(h) can be expressed as **Production - Consumption**. The human function has a consequence. That consequence is called **Surplus**. The values of **Surplus**, which can be positive, negative, or zero, are discussed below.

We have been created to require regular access to food and water to survive. Nature, as the expression of the creation, is the source of that food and water. But since the Fall, such provision comes from work—"the sweat of our brow." (Genesis 3:19) Thus, humankind today reports to jobs of all

---

[27] Marcelo Sanchez Sorondo and Veerabhadran Ramanathan, "Pursuit of Integral Ecology," *Science*, May 13, 2016, 747.

descriptions in order to obtain food and drink for themselves and their families.

The human function $f(h)$ is a general statement of all humanity. A further refinement of the function would be that portion of humanity called to follow Jesus Christ as their Lord and Savior. This Christian subset is designated by $f(h_c)$ and identified by their obedience to the teachings of the Bible. While some in the secular world form their consumption preferences around mantras such as "The one who dies with the most toys wins" or "I once was/Now I am not/And I don't care," noted on ancient Roman tombstones, the Christian will be guided by the teachings of Jesus.

The Biblical motifs of production, consumption, and **surplus** thread themselves through scripture from the beginning to the end. Production is the result of productivity—the inclination and capacity to produce through work. It originates with God's work in completing the creation, incorporates humankind through the story of the Fall, and is displayed again and again from Abraham to Moses. Jesus divinely demonstrates it with wine and fish on multiple occasions in the New Testament. And all this is under the watchful eye of our omniscient God when he commends in Revelation 2:2, "I know your deeds, your hard work, and your perseverance."

The Bible's motif on consumption is cautionary. It has been commented on for centuries. John Chrysostom in his late fourth-century homily on wealth and poverty stated,

> Our use of earthly and natural goods must be oriented toward higher and spiritual goods. Another way of saying this is that our desires and consumption must be rightly ordered: " ...let us accustom ourselves to eat only enough to live, not enough to be distracted and weighed down. For we were not born, we do not live, in order to eat and drink; but we eat in order to leave (sic). At the beginning life was not made for eating, but eating for life. But we, as if we had come into the world for this purpose, spend everything for eating" (27–28).[28]

Surplus is the positive difference between production and consumption.

---

[28] Jordan J. Ballor, "John Chrysostom, on Wealth and Poverty, Part 1," in *Acton Institute Powerblog* (Acton Institute, 2007).

It is not always guaranteed, and its lack is called a famine or drought. Extended droughts and famine cause significant numbers of people to die. A stasis of only enough food and water to support a certain population number has not been demonstrated for extended periods. Growing families require more food and water than that required by only the parents. Since babies cannot produce, it is up to the parents to produce more than they themselves consume—a **surplus**. That **surplus** is used to feed the new arrivals until they can become productive. The Abramic and Noahic covenants contain not just that the people of God will grow, but that God will make available a **surplus** to support that growth. They will flourish in both numbers and abundance. God's promise trumped Thomas Malthus, the Enlightenment economist, who said that unchecked exponential human reproduction would only maintain equilibrium with arithmetic food production through war, famine, pestilence, and catastrophe.[29]

Over time, humans learned to barter their **surplus** food stocks for stores of value that could be preserved and exchanged for food in challenging times. The novella of Joseph shows how divine inspiration caused him to preserve food stocks to be available for distribution and barter at a future date. While Joseph dealt with stored food, longer stores of value have evolved using precious metal coins, then paper legal tender, and now computer binary bits reflecting balances on credit cards and in bank accounts. These stores of value have become known as wealth. Those who control the distribution of **surplus** are called "wealthy."

The continuing wealthy meme, or caricature, of hands scooping up gold coins from a stash in an open chest reflects how out of date our conversation on wealth is. For instance, cached **surplus** can also be represented by leisure time. The leisure time to spend on things other than farming—education, for example. Few are the times since the nineteenth century that students must leave school to help bring in the harvest. The growing **surplus** is what fuels higher education (including seminaries). Time away from farming (or other work) to obtain food provides for refreshment, hobbies, and charitable service. This is how God intends us to flourish, not just survive.

The abstract idea that time away from work could improve the human experience was termed σχολή (schole) in Greek and *otium* in Latin—a conceptual idea highly prized by Greek and Roman philosophers. And the

---

[29] T. R. Malthus, *Additions to an Essay on the Principle of Population*, 1st ed. (Georgetown: C. Cruickshank, 1831).

identification of who is wealthy morphs with such intangibles as well to anyone who controls or influences the distribution of **surplus**. The wealthy include people who allocate leisure applications. They decide scholarships, fill endowed chairs, grant sabbaticals, and pay honorariums. They have been placed in such positions of power because they have the gift of productive disbursement of **surplus**.

The same can be said of corporate leaders, government bureaucrats, NGO presidents, church staff, and others who lead organizational endeavors. Because of their determinations over **surplus** disbursements, they all have power over the direction and quality of other people's lives—and earn the wealthy appellation or label.

The Roman Catholic Church—as well as other theological enclaves—have come to respect the positive aspects of **surplus** and those who distribute it. Coming from the theological side of the discussion, they are learning very different and new ways to describe wealth.

Statements in recent history, though clearly not universal, show dramatic movement in the faith/wealth dialogue. Examples include the declaration "Sin makes work an ambiguous reality. It is both a noble expression of human creation in the image of God, and, because of the curse, a painful testimony to human estrangement from God," the "Oxford Declaration on Christian Faith and Economics 1990," a more recent declaration "Wealth creation is a holy calling and a God-given gift that is commended in the Bible," the Lausanne Movement and Business as Mission Global: *The Role of Wealth Creation for Holistic Transformation 2017.*

But in these religious leaders' urgency to have businessmen hear their new perspective on the positives of wealth, they have muted some of their historical biblical concerns on those who manage it. They have not forgotten the sulfur aroma of James 5; they simply have not yet formulated a healthy way to include such condemnations into the new enlightened dialogue. That is why the theological/economic bridge on wealth cannot yet be completed.

James (3:11) and Paul (1 Timothy 6:9) echo Jesus when they caution not to be a teacher or a wealthy person (although one certainly does not imply the other). In both instances, the caution is that they will be judged with greater scrutiny. And that is because both have greater responsibility because of their power to influence lives. The authority to disburse **surplus** changes lives—and that is power. That power can create a toxic and corrosive atmosphere for those who operate in it. It can warp idealistic intentions, rationalize error, and bring disease to the soul. At the inspiration of the great philologist Eugene

Peterson, I have coined the word *plutogenics* as the disease of the soul prevalent to those that are subject to the atmosphere of wealth. This is the subject of a later chapter.

The consequences of *plutogenics* are real and can be fatal. It can cause suffering and death in this life as well as for eternity. Like other sinners, the wealthy can be redeemed, as Jesus noted in response to that very question from his disciples. God's requirements for the wealthy are just as they are for teachers. Some wealthy are spiritually healthy, but many of them are not. To detect illness, you must first be able to recognize the symptoms. The symptoms of *plutogenics* include avarice, gluttony, drunkenness, arrogance, hoarding, and separation. These will be addressed in a later chapter. Only the grace of God is sufficient to cure such ills. It falls on the leaders of the church to emulate the Great Physician in making such grace known and accepted by those who suffer from the malady.

An absolute mandate of God's plan is sustainable **surplus**. The growth of the church has not come from a one-time distribution event of **surplus**. The growth of the church requires a sustained growing **surplus** and spiritually healthy people to distribute it. Those facts need to be made clear by the church in a loud, clear, stentorian voice. At the same time, the church needs to minister to those wounded or weakened by that endeavor to continue building the Body of Christ with Jesus as its head.

5
PRODUCTION—THE FIRST PART OF THE HUMAN FUNCTION $f(h)$

Six days you shall labor and do all your work.

—Exodus 20:9 (NIV)

In this chapter, we examine the concept and biblical guidance regarding production as the first variable of the human function $f(h)$.

PRODUCTION IN ECONOMICS AND THEOLOGY

The ability to produce is called *productivity*; it requires work. It is a divine quality expressed in God's first actions. God began his production process *ex nihilo*, which in Latin means "from nothing." Diligent efforts in science to reverse engineer the act of creation has produced an interesting theory of singularity. Although unable to help with where the singularity came from or what initiated its first action, it creates awe in the imagination of how the entire universe could have proceeded from such a microscopic seminal event. The more humankind explores theories of creation, the more magnificent, intricate, and divine it appears.

God also created humankind in his own image. He declared all of this production "good." His creation contains the further *means of production* that humans would subsequently use and exchange for their sustenance.

Humans possess the ability to produce and reproduce as part of God's plan. Having children—reproduction—is a blessing from God and part of the human function $f(h)$. That implies that the human function $f(h)$ must also produce ever-increasing amounts of food to support a growing population. As pointed out earlier, Thomas Malthus (1766–1823) concluded that since unchecked human population grows geometrically and food production, at that time, grew arithmetically, only war, pestilence, and calamity could bring them back into balance.

This harsh worldview caused his economics to be called the "dismal science." Although Malthus could not foresee the productivity gains that have caused his paradigm to be reassessed, the relationship of an ever-increasing food supply to support an ever-increasing population remains intact. Food must first be produced to maintain human viability.

As intuitively obvious as such a statement might seem, the notion that production was a prerequisite to consumption has been challenged by modern economists. Keynesian followers (John Maynard Keynes 1883–1946) argue that an increase in aggregate demand will increase aggregate supply—consumption precedes production. Say's Law (Jean-Baptiste Say 1767–1832), on the other hand, states that aggregate supply stimulates aggregate demand—production precedes consumption.

Who is correct? This debate generates its heartiest arguments when applied to today's universally complex economy with substantial markets for advanced goods, which have lost their seeming connection to food. And yet, Say's earlier proposition is gaining more contemporary traction. The world's economy already produces sufficient food for all its people. The danger of famine and starvation can be addressed through charity and organizations that provide worldwide distribution.

Unfortunately, the last leg of that distribution must go through local political/military hegemony. Corrupt forces often stifle food's free distribution. The power of food distribution is weaponized to continue the subjugation of the hungry. Thus, while sufficient food stockpiles exist, famine still threatens because of human corruption and failure.

The first-world economies that are surfeit in food focus on inflation and employment as the parameters for when to turn the valves and pull the levers of outside adjustment. Such national economies dominate the total economy of the world today. The economy of today is not reflective of the Levantine economy in the times of the Old and New Testaments. If we are to understand the teachings of Jesus and the Bible, we must understand the economy within which he taught and use an economic model that reflects it.

As expressed previously, I believe the praxeology method, which studies *a priori* preferences and existential circumstances to predict future economic action, is the most reliable. It finds its threads originating from theologians and philosophers such as Thomas Aquinas (1225–1274) and Claude Frédéric Bastiat (1801–1850). They felt that economics must reflect its precursors—life, liberty, and property. There are very many subsequent contributors who built on that premise.

Carl Menger (1840–1921) is generally credited with organizing and expanding its principles to form the Austrian School of Economics. A recent observation of the school states, "An existential fact of human existence is that we can only increase our stock of consumption goods by producing them. This in turn implies a fundamental economic principle: 'we produce in order to consume.'"[30]

The Austrian model arrives at this by the observation of praxis in the real world. That observation is the same expression contained in the human function $f(h)$. In agreement with the Austrian observation, we have placed our economic model on a rational footing with production as its first action. Human work is a necessary but not sufficient condition to accomplish production. Production results from work when it has God's blessing. With that in mind, we are now able to return to the Bible to see what it has to say about production and work.

THE BIBLE ON PRODUCTION AND WORK

In the beginning, God was the first mover and did the work that produced the creation. Genesis 2:3 states, "Then God blessed the seventh day and made it holy, because on it he rested from all the *work* of creating that he had done" (NIV). The Hebrew word in the Masoretic text is הַמְּלָאכָה (*melakah*: occupation, work), which connotes a purposeful effort but not one of drudgery or punishing labor.

Later, Genesis 2:15 says, "The LORD God took the man and put him in the Garden of Eden to *work* it and take care of it."[31] The Hebrew word here is עָבַד (*abad*: to work, serve). Again, while the activity is directed, it is not

---

[30] Ritenour, 163.
[31] Kenneth L. Barker, ed. *Zondervan Niv Study Bible* (Grand Rapids: Zondervan, 2008).

drudgery or punishment. Some have interpreted that the directed activity "gives man purpose," inferring that being unemployed can have a deleterious effect on a person's self-esteem.[32] Adam's purpose in this case would be to cultivate the garden and make it even more productive.

But finally, in Genesis 3:17, as a result of human defiance, God declares, "Cursed is the ground because of you; through *painful toil* you will eat food from it all the days of your life." "Painful toil" now replaces "work" as the requirement for Adam to initiate his human function. The Hebrew word וּבְעֶצֶב (*itstsabon*: a pain, toil) reflects the consequential change. Some see this allegorically as "the primal couple have left the magical garden of their childhood and their innocence and entered into the harsh world of adulthood and its painful realities."[33]

But the human function itself continued beyond Adam and Eve. God's plan remained that humans were still expected to multiply and flourish. Jeremiah 29:11 would later reaffirm, "'For I know the plans I have for you,' declares the LORD, 'plans to prosper you and not to harm you, plans to give you hope and a future.'"[34]

The "you" he was speaking to was the successive generations who would leave their families and enter into the real world under their own power to work and sustain themselves. What needs to be inculcated is that their efforts require God's blessing to flourish. This was known from the earliest days of the Jewish patriarchs. It was their blessing, which provided the continuity of God's covenant with Abraham. Each successive generation sought that blessing. The blessing of a patriarch invoked God's part in production as exemplified by the blessing of Isaac to Jacob in Genesis 27:28:

> Therefore may God give you Of the dew of heaven, Of the fatness of the earth, And plenty of grain and wine[35]

As can be seen from the blessing, productivity was initially tied generically to land for crops and sustaining husbandry. But as Moses led the Exodus

---

[32] Frederick Dale Bruner, *Matthew, a Commentary*, vol. 2 (Dallas: Word Publishing, 1990), 724.

[33] Berlin and others, 17–8.

[34] Barker, ed.

[35] Earl D. Th.D. Radmacher, ed. *The Nkjv Study Bible*, 2nd ed. (Nashville: Thomas Nelson, Inc., 2007).

to the Promised Land, the Hebrew economic teachings would morph to specifically address the private ownership of land. This is important for two reasons: productivity and exchange. Why would God, "whose justice would be a light to the nations," direct his chosen people to individual land ownership rather than a communal nomadic life? Agricultural productivity requires work, and work is greatly affected by the concept of private property.

First, we address the productivity of private ownership. Since ancient Greek times, private property was seen to better foster progress due to greater productivity. Aristotle noted that "goods that are owned by a large number of people receive little care. People are inclined to consider chiefly their own interest and are apt to neglect a duty that they expect others to fulfill."[36] Thus, Moses would ultimately assign ownership of the Promised Land to individual tribes who would further assign them to households. He knew that the household, led by the patriarch, would best correlate ownership with responsibility.

But Moses did not lose the perspective that individual effort was vital to God's ongoing plans for humankind. Psalm 90, attributed to Moses, states, "May the favor of the Lord our God rest on us; establish the *work* of our hands for us—yes, establish the *work* of our hands."[37] The Hebrew word employed here is מַעֲשֵׂה (*maaseh*: a deed, work). This is the word used when work has a relationship to God—for his glory or for his purpose. Moses concludes it is that "work of our hands" that is to prosper as part of God's enduring plan and implores God's blessing on it.[38]

Moses also ties our work to our very significance and our contribution to future generations. The third section of the *Tanakh* (Hebrew Bible) is known as the *Ketuvim,* meaning "Writings." Proverbs is contained in both the Hebrew *Ketuvim* and the Christian Old Testament and is viewed as divinely inspired both by Jews and Christians. They both see the book of Proverbs "containing insight, good sense, and the hard-fought experience of those that have gone before—the kind of guidance that helps us grow up, get along in society, and hold a job"[39].

Proverbs' comments on work can be broken down into two segments

---

[36] Henry William Spiegel, *The Growth of Economic Thought* (Englewood Cliffs: Prentice-Hall, 1971), 13.

[37] Barker, ed.

[38] Berlin and others, 1385.

[39] Radmacher, ed., 963.

reinforcing a single idea—working is good; not working is bad. Proverbs 12:11 says that working the land will provide abundant food. Proverbs 6:10–12 warns that a lack of work brings poverty. Proverbs 12:24 says that conscientious workers can ultimately work for themselves, while derelict workers will be forced to work by others. Proverbs 14:23 says that actual hard work pays off while only talking about it leads to poverty. Proverbs 16:3 reaffirms that. If you work for God's glory, he will guide your path.

It is clear that Proverbs not only encourages work but sees it as essential to the success of the human function $f(h)$. This explains why we can feel such fulfillment in our work. It is part of God's plan and meaning for our lives.

We now turn to the New Testament to examine the life and teachings of Jesus for what he would have us understand about work and productivity and their role in the human function $f(h)$.

During the period of Jesus's ministry, he lived and taught those who would listen to him every day of the week. He taught them in the fields, in their homes, and in places of worship. Frequently, he would teach using parables. "Parables are short fictitious stories contained within a popularly understood earthly setting projecting a heavenly meaning."[40]

In such parables, we are presented with economic principles from which the divine truth emanates. Jesus's presentations of economic settings such as vineyards, fields and storehouses and their operations provide important economic context *in situ*. It is from these principles and context that we will draw our conclusions of what Jesus has to say about work and productivity.

MATTHEW 20:1–16—THE PARABLE OF THE LABORERS

This parable has a single main theological point, which is emphasized by an *inclusio* of Matthew 19:28 and Matthew 20:16, that "the last shall be first and the first shall be last" in heaven. This point has been hermeneutically applied to Jews/Gentiles, Pharisees/Jews, Jewish Christians/Gentiles, young/old, and mainline churches/churches with newer approaches, among others. The divine probity of the parable is the realm of the theologian.

Proleptically, we acknowledge that Jesus's purpose for the parable is to describe heaven. It is his purpose as well in other Matthean parables, including the Parable of the Two Kinds of Sons (21:28–32) and the Parable of the Two

---

[40] Evans and Porter, 909.

Kinds of Farmers (21:33–46). But an economist, too, can glean principles from these parables that are valuable from an economic perspective.

The earthly context of each of these parables is a plausible conversation or setting. In each of the settings different actions by the participants are possible, resulting in potentially different outcomes. The setting itself does not prevent the possibility of right relationships to manifest. The participants may or may not reflect the love Jesus teaches, but that is not because Jesus has placed them in a specious situation. They act out of their own internal motivations.

Thus, the following economic observations can be relied on as valid. The search for productivity is the prime mover in the story. All of the economic concepts such as householders hiring day laborers, people aspiring to work, use of a denarius (money) for exchange, fair wages, mutually agreed contracts, and the discretionary use of private property are employed toward that end. Jesus is content to provide his important theological lesson in a pericope about a householder legitimately seeking to make his land productive. Jesus, we conclude, *de facto* approves of productivity and contemporaneous economic actions to achieve it.

MATTHEW 25:14–30—THE PARABLE OF THE TALENTS (MARK 13:34, LUKE 19:11–27)

Approaching Jerusalem, Jesus is aware that his close disciples still expect temporal messianic action upon their arrival. He stops to tell them parables that portray him leaving for an extended period but that they must remain to faithfully carry out his work. Many commentators limit their interpretation to its theology.[41]

Others additionally find some practical instruction in these similar parables found in all three synoptic gospels. They conclude Christians also remain faithful by employing their resources while patiently awaiting the return and assessment of the Lord. A commentator calling the same parable, "On the Watch" (Mark 13:34–37), concludes, "We are like men who know

---

[41] Norval Geldenhuys, *Commentary on the Gospel of Luke*, New London Commentary on the New Testament (London: Marshall, Morgan and Scott, 1971), 473–8.

that their master will come but who do not know when. ... But it does mean that day by day our work must be completed and done."[42]

The idea that work is expected of us, even in his absence, shows the value of productivity in Jesus's eyes. It also infers that the human function $f(h)$ is to continue until his return. The parables in Matthew and Luke speak richly about the quality of the work expected and the difference in productivity and reward such excellent work can bring. Matthew 25:14–30 is entitled "The Parable of the Talents" and Luke 19:11–27 is entitled "The Kingship Parable." Since both of these parables are explained in detailed economic terms, it may be useful for us to compare and contrast them to better extract their importance to the human function $f(h)$ and production in particular.

While both parables set the premise as an extremely powerful and wealthy person charging his followers to be productive in his absence, Luke ties the owner's trip to a political objective while Matthew does not state the purpose of the owner's travel. Many see Luke's narrative as parallel to that of Archelaus, son of Herod the Great, upon his father's death as reported by Josephus.[43] The differences in the charge by the departing patron are interesting.

In Matthew, the patron already knows the capabilities of his three servants and makes the corresponding assignments (*kata ten idian dynamic*: according to their own ability). The described action of the servant given five talents begins at once. Using the word Εὐθέως (*eutheos*: immediately), he runs off abruptly anxious to get started.

In Luke, the patron selects ten subjects and hands out an equal assignment to each indicating a greater diversification of the risk amongst a larger number of unproven performers. While he only assesses three, the outcome is the same. A few people will be outstanding producers, some will be adequate producers, and some will be poor producers.

There are several key takeaways here. Excellence in work is of primary value to the employer. Secondly, people have different abilities and motivations toward work. These form a similitude regarding God's expectation of, and reward for, the excellent work and production of some in support of the human function $f(h)$. A growing **surplus** cannot be achieved without sustained excellence in production and a constant monitoring of consumption.

The amounts of money entrusted between the two parables were

---

[42] William Barclay, *The Gospel of Mark*, 2nd ed. (Philadelphia: Westminster Press, 1957), 337.

[43] Geldenhuys, 477.

substantially different—the eight talents in Matthew versus a total of 10 minas in Luke. A mina was a coin equal to 100 denarii or one hundred man-days of work. A talent equaled 60 minas or 6,000 man-days of work from a single worker (about sixteen years of work). While five talents represented about eighty years of work.

Matthew was dealing in very large sums. The top performers returned 10 talents in Matthew and 11 minas in Luke. Despite the substantially larger sums in Matthew, high achievers were praised and rewarded with more responsibility in both parables—capital in the case of Matthew and political position in the case of Luke.

We find another interesting commonality in these two parables. Jesus praises productivity through business transactions, not agriculture. The master in Matthew does not give specific instructions to his subordinates in how to employ the capital but leaves it to their ingenuity. In Luke, he tells them πραγματεύομαι (*pragmateuomai*: to do business, trade). There is an acknowledged element of risk involved. Trading over long distances, especially by sea, were seen as high-risk business ventures. But they paid off if "your ship came in."

The ten-time return reported in the Luke parable is an amiable goal for a current-day venture capitalist. Indeed, when the top performer in Matthew reports to the master that he doubled his capital, he uses the Greek word κερδανή (*kerdainó*: to gain, to profit) to indicate that he took a risk, which could have resulted in a loss. Both high producers had the skill to navigate a high-risk business environment and to do well. For this, the masters provide the highest accolades, verbally praising them in front of their peers.

Additionally, they were both put in charge of more capital. While some see the reward in Luke to be only of a political nature, a primary responsibility of a political appointee over cities was to see that taxes and tribute were collected. They would become rich by deducting a portion of the tribute/taxes. On the parable in Matthew, everyone agrees as to its economic focus. Theologian F. Dale Bruner even notes, "Entrepreneurial business comes out well in the Parable of the Talents."[44]

Too often, theologians look down on work and those who achieve greatly through it because they see it as simply chasing riches. Those who subscribe to that point of view should look more closely at these two parables. Bruner further comments, "When Christians acknowledge the priority of God's

---

[44] Bruner, 905.

work, they may rejoice in the posteriority of their work. There is a joy in work here that should not be depressed by a heavy-handed spirituality. *Jesus wants disciples to feel good about their work.*[45] The master provided an opportunity for those not skilled in business to at least obtain a return by depositing the money in a "bank." Now we should be careful that the literal translation of τράπεζα (*trapeza*: a table) is "table-men" who were money changers—a very extensive business during the Roman occupation period. Jesus severely chastises his charges for not doing even that and only hiding the capital given to them.

Jesus does not reward idle capital—it is to be put to work. It is dead money. It doesn't circulate. It is illiquid and not available for earning a return. The hard lesson found in both parables is that those with nothing will have even that taken away from them. While some theologians see this as purely an allegorical statement of a Christian's need to grow in faith or lose it, economists and several commentators see it in economic terms. Those who do not practice and hone their craft will even lose their ability to do it at all. The opportunities for future work will then go to the more diligent.[46]

The Gospel of John is different in several important ways from the synoptic gospels of Matthew, Mark, and Luke. Its selections from the ministry of Jesus emphasize his attributes as the Messiah and the Son of God in order "that believing, you may have life in His name."[47] Accepting that premise, we look for Jesus's thoughts on productivity and work in his direct discourse. Because these discussions derive from his daily actions they should resonate in our everyday lives. We find him discussing work in John 5. On a Sabbath, a paralytic is frustrated by his inability to reach the healing waters of the pool at Bethesda in time to be healed. Jesus has pity on the man and heals him.

Jesus is subsequently criticized by the Jews for healing, that is working, on the Sabbath. In his defense Jesus said to them, "My Father is always at his work to this very day, and I too am working." Jesus says some significant things here. First with respect to God (my father) he uses the Greek word ἐργάζεται (*ergazetai*: is working) in the present indicative tense.

He is saying that God is continually at work even in the present, for all time. Working is an attribute of God and it is good. Jesus is pleased to assume

---

[45] Ibid., 906, emphasis mine.

[46] Charles John Ellicott, *Ellicot's Bible Commentary*, ed. PhD Donald N. Bowdle, ThD (Grand Rapids: Zondervan Publishing House, 1971), 743.

[47] Radmacher, ed., John 20:31.

the same mantel when he says, "And I am working too." It is the intent of the Gospel of John that we reflect this divine trait of working. Paul says this is reflected in the lives of the Apostles when he testifies that we "work hard with our own hands."[48] In Colossians 3:23, he exhorts us to do even better, to "work at it with all your heart, as working for the Lord, not for human masters." He reminds us that if our work reflects our gift to the Lord he will bless it. John confirms God is watching when he says in Revelation 2:2, "I know your deeds, your hard work and your perseverance."

Work and productivity are intertwined. But the third strand of God's blessing is necessary for them to be successful. Scripture says that success should always be recognized by offering the first fruits, yearlings, and coins to God as a recognition that he first gave to us.

There are many moving stories of how young people have heard God call them to the work of ministry. To know that God has a personal interest in what you do is an empowering and motivating feeling. It makes you more industrious and focused on what you do. It makes you better at your job. Does God call young people to be accountants or farmers or musicians? I think he does. It is manifest in the different gifts he gives each individual and the yearning in their heart to develop that gift.

I was told an apocryphal story by Leighton Ford, who is a close ministry associate of Billy Graham and married to Jean Graham Ford. He said that, one day, Billy and his brother were taking a break on the family dairy farm near Charlotte, North Carolina. Lying side by side on the grass and looking up at the blue sky with puffy white clouds, Billy suddenly pointed to a cloud formation.

"Mel, do you see that? In the clouds—G P T G. God is calling me to Go, Preach, The, Gospel!"

Melvin, quickly acknowledging the clouds, replied, "No he is not. He is telling us to Go, Plow, The, Ground." I believe they were both right and interpreted the clouds correctly.

Melvin lived a very productive farm life using it to build the Kingdom of God. And of course, God used Billy mightily to bring new members into the Kingdom.

God speaks to each of us according to our gifts. And he has a plan for us in using those gifts to his great glory. We should be energized and motivated by that thought. Rick Warren emphasizes this point, saying,

---

[48] Ibid., 1 Cor 4:12.

> Growing up, you may have thought that being "called" by God was something only missionaries, pastors, nuns, and other "full-time" church workers experienced, but the Bible says every Christian is called to service.[49]

No matter how large and complex the world's economy becomes, it will require human effort to sustain it and will continue to require God's blessing to achieve the purpose He intends. In contemporary times, many have lost the connection that God is there to bless our work no matter how far from agriculture it has evolved.

Too many pastors only make the connection of God's blessing on our work when the offering plate is passed. They forget that all of our work, all of the time, is done for the glory of God. Such gifts which are recognized in the secular world with promotions and titles should not be shunned by the church. "Before God created you, he decided what role he wanted you to play on earth. He planned exactly how he wanted you to serve him, and then he shaped you for those tasks."[50]

The church should celebrate such shaping for the glory of God. God has not abandoned his desire that humanity grow and flourish. He has not abandoned us to pursue our work without him. There are no secular days of the week for God's people. Some people are "good at building a business, making deals or sales, and reaping a profit. If you have this business ability, you should be using it for God's glory."[51] While we worship communally on Sundays, we worship individually at work on other days.

Pastors, who understand the scripture's call to productivity, help find work for unemployed congregants. They pray for God's blessing on those who work hard to produce. And they publicly recognize the achievements and generosity of those who have been successful.

---

[49] Rick Warren, *The Purpose Driven® Life: What on Earth Am I Here For?* (Philadelphia: Running Press Book Publishers, 2003), loc. 3258, Kindle.

[50] Ibid., loc. 3339, Kindle.

[51] Ibid., loc. 3466, Kindle.

6
CONSUMPTION—THE SECOND PART OF THE HUMAN FUNCTION f(h)

You will eat the fruit of your labor;
blessings and prosperity will be yours.

—Psalm 128:2 (NIV)

In this chapter, we examine the second variable of the human function f(h) from a scientific and biblical perspective.

CONSUMPTION IN ECONOMICS AND THEOLOGY

As stated in the chapter on the human function f(h), the component of consumption is all about food. Humankind's most continuously proximate need is sustenance—food and water. Every day, we need a plan for food and water. Routines can sometimes mask this planning. But if we go without food or drink beyond normal periods, our bodies send us recognizable signals to focus our attention on the need. Our very survival depends on these signals. A rough rule of thumb is that a person dies after three days without water and three weeks without food. Deprivation of either food or water can get very uncomfortable much sooner than that.

Maslow's *Hierarchy of Needs* is a theory that attempts to explain human motivation. According to Maslow, humans' first and primary motivation is to satisfy biological needs including hunger and thirst. God knew this before Maslow because that is the way he created us. He knew what we would need to sustain ourselves. Genesis 2:8–9 tells us, "Now the Lord God had planted a garden in the east, in Eden; and there he put the man he had formed. The Lord God made all kinds of trees grow out of the ground—trees that were pleasing to the eye and good for food." It also says that he purposely planted the garden where a river would provide water for the trees and Adam. But as previously pointed out, due to Adam and Eve's sin, God's free provision of this food and water would require work to procure in the future.

Despite the new requirement of toil, humankind's primary motivation would become the cultivating of fields and the digging of wells. The human function $f(h)$ reflects this primary motivation. The first postulate of the economist Thomas Malthus was "that food is necessary to the existence of man."[52] We previously noted that he effectively connected the availability of food to the size and growth of human population. God implied to Abraham that sufficient food would be available such that "I will make of you a great nation, and I will bless you and make your name great, so that you will be a blessing."[53]

We previously highlighted Ritenour's statement that "an existential fact of human existence is that we can only increase our stock of consumption goods by producing them. This in turn implies a fundamental economic principle: 'we produce in order to consume.'" This statement within the Austrian school of economics implies a broader definition of consumption than just food. But no matter how complex an economy grows, food still remains our first concern. This has been demonstrated many times throughout history as people have been willing to trade all of their possessions for the acquisition of food and water.

Is Christian consumption all about ascetic calorie counting and fasting? Are we called to a perpetual life of Lent where we deny ourselves the benefice of the creation? Are we meant to toil and consume in dreariness? The writer of Ecclesiastes argues no. To make his point, he repeats five times that we should experience enjoyment in this life through eating and drinking. We should find satisfaction in our toil by partaking of its harvest. And we should acknowledge the bounty and the ability to enjoy it as a gift of God. His words

---

[52] T. R. Malthus, *An Essay on the Principle of Population*, Everyman's University Library (London: J. M. Dent, 1973), loc. 84, Kindle.

[53] Radmacher, ed., Genesis 12:2.

become exhortative in Ecclesiastes 9:7 when he says, "Go, eat your food with gladness, and drink your wine with a joyful heart, for God has already approved what you do."

Jesus found it most appropriate to enjoy food and drink socially. He enhanced weddings, taught using feasts as examples, and did some of his most important work at meals in the homes of others. Such an approach to ministry was so apparent that even devout followers asked him for clarification. It is important enough that it is addressed in all three synoptic gospels. Mark 2:19 notes His consistent answer was a question, "Can the wedding guests fast while the bridegroom is with them?" (ESV).

Christians understand that he was speaking of himself. He pointed out that there would be a time for fasting in the days that the bridegroom is taken away. Fasting can be a very meaningful religious exercise and experience. It can commemorate his passion and crucifixion. But Christians also understand that he was resurrected to join his bride, the church, to form one body with Christ as the head. We celebrate that reunion as a perpetual wedding feast each time we partake of bread and wine—not just during religious observances. We should celebrate community get-togethers, birthdays, anniversaries, and every other social gathering with the bounty of the creation in the knowledge that Jesus is with us.

But the Bible and science also warns us about our diet. It should be balanced and proportionate. Early on in history, gluttony and drunkenness were seen as threats to one's health by bringing on gout and delirium. Your chances of getting gout are higher if you are overweight, drink too much alcohol, or eat too much meat and fish. A concentration of these foods can build uric acid in the blood, causing a painful type of arthritis.[54]

Historically, such foods have been relatively expensive and thus generated the observation that gout was the "rich man's disease." In modern times, nutrition has become the subject of collegiate study and an important growth industry for improving health and vitality. The absolute need for a variety of foods, eaten in moderation, will help us understand the Bible's teaching on consumption using food and water as a surrogate.

---

[54] Mayo Clinic Staff, "Nutrition and Healthy Eating," Mayo Clinic, https://www.mayoclinic.org/healthy-lifestyle/nutrition-and-healthy-eating/in-depth/gout-diet/art-20048524, accessed 2017.

THE BIBLE ON CONSUMPTION

The Old Testament

Few illustrations in the Bible show God's understanding of the human need and provision for food and water so clearly as the book of Exodus. God told Moses that the priority was to move the Jews out of Egypt quickly. That meant that they were to be fully fed by a lamb sacrifice the evening of Passover and ready to go. The flocks had to be gathered and the bread could not wait for leavening. A population estimated possibly as high as 2.5 million men, women and children had to be ready to go with less than an hour's notice.[55]

As critical as the departure was, God knew they needed food to accomplish the task. They left with full stomachs, herds of animals, and unleavened bread. In Exodus 16, we are told that after two months their food was running out. Being led into a wilderness with no prospects in sight, they complained to Moses that they would rather have stayed slaves in Egypt then to starve free in the wilderness. Realizing that food was of first priority if they were to make it to the Promised Land, God provided a continuing source of food in terms of quail and manna for the next forty years.

The lack of food humbles humans and reminds them of their frailty and dependence on God. Moses reminds them in Deuteronomy 8:3, "He humbled you, causing you to hunger and then feeding you with manna, which neither you nor your ancestors had known, to teach you that man does not live on bread alone but on every word that comes from the mouth of the Lord."

Necessarily, God also provided water when the people could not. The subject of water is treated in Genesis 17. As the people moved from the Wilderness of Sin, water became beyond their capability to find. Upon instruction from God, Moses took his staff to Horeb, where he was to strike a rock. His action in front of witnesses caused water to flow. The people received another demonstration that God would provide their requirements for water even when they could not. This provision of water would be again documented many years later in Numbers 20, although this time, Moses would claim the achievement rather than giving the glory to God. Because he assumed God's glory, Moses was prevented from entering the Promised Land.

The Old Testament is equally insistent that too much food or drink is bad

---

[55] Berlin and others, 129, note 35–36.

for your physical health as well as your spiritual well-being. Proverbs 23:20 cautions, "Do not be with heavy drinkers of wine, Or with gluttonous eaters of meat."[56] Later, Proverb 28:7 cautions, "He who keeps the law is a discerning son, But he who is a companion of gluttons humiliates his father."[57]

But it is Proverbs 30:9 that anticipates the daily bread request as part of the Lord's Prayer. There is a reason for moderation in our consumption. As it states, "Lest I be full and deny *You,* And say, "Who *is* the LORD?" Or lest I be poor and steal, And profane the name of my God."[58]

The New Testament

Early in the New Testament all three synoptic gospels have Jesus driven by the spirit into the wilderness where he does not eat for forty days. By putting himself *in extremis,* he both demonstrates his humanity and makes himself subject to terrible temptation by the devil. Taunted to turn stones into bread, Jesus quotes Deuteronomy 8:3, "not by bread alone ..." Bruner notes,

> Both Jesus and the Scripture he cites are too realistic to say "not by bread at all." Man lives by bread at least. We must have bread to live. Jesus teaches us to pray for it (6:11), says the Father knows we must have it (6:32), and even promises that where God's kingdom is sought first, bread, too, will be brought us (6:33b)."[59]

At later times in the gospels, Jesus will actually provide food and wine to large groups who are without. This is not to miss the crucial theological point that true life is much more than just eating and ultimately depends on "consuming" the words of the Lord as well. Food is a necessary but not sufficient condition for the abundant life offered to followers of Jesus.

While they cannot dispute his ability to produce food and drink, the Pharisees attack him on the issue of consumption. They know that scripture

---

[56] Zondervan Publishing House, *Nasb Compact Reference Bible: New American Standard Bible* (Grand Rapids: Zondervan Pub. House, 2000).

[57] Ibid.

[58] Radmacher, ed.

[59] Frederick Dale Bruner, *The Christbook: A Historical/Theological Commentary* (Waco: Word Books, 1987), 106.

has addressed the manner and amount of food that is to be eaten. Now they try to compare and contrast the actions of John the Baptist with Jesus expecting that they both cannot be right. Jesus notes this in Matthew 11, saying, "For John came neither eating nor drinking, and they say, 'He has a demon.' The Son of Man came eating and drinking, and they say, 'Here is a glutton and a drunkard, a friend of tax collectors and sinners.' But wisdom is proved right by her deeds."[60]

Clearly neither of the ends of the spectrum of consumption as described, "neither eating or drinking" and "a glutton and a drunkard," were exhibited by John or Jesus. John ate and Jesus was not a glutton. But the truth of Jesus's reply is found in his conclusion that "wisdom is proved right by her deeds." Wisdom, the right way of life, is present in both John's and Jesus's consumption, because they are neither at the extremes of the spectrum and yet their consumption is sufficient for their ministries (deeds).

Dr. Martin Luther King Jr. saw a connection between consumption and our need for recognition as expressed in Mark 10. The kind of recognition that John and James request from Jesus when they ask to sit on his left and right when he comes into glory. King calls it a "kind of drum major instinct—a desire to be out front, a desire to lead the parade, a desire to be first. And it is something that runs the whole gamut of life."[61] He points out that this very strong instinct found in all of us is perverted in conspicuous consumption.

> Now the presence of this instinct explains why we are so often taken by advertisers. You know, those gentlemen of massive verbal persuasion. And they have a way of saying things to you that kind of gets you into buying. In order to be a man of distinction, you must drink this whiskey. In order to make your neighbors envious, you must drive this type of car. (*Make it plain*) In order to be lovely to love you must wear this kind of lipstick or this kind of perfume. And you know, before you know it, you're just buying that stuff.[62]

---

[60] Radmacher, ed.

[61] Martin Luther King, Clayborne Carson, and Peter C. Holloran, *A Knock at Midnight : Inspiration from the Great Sermons of Reverend Martin Luther King, Jr* (London: Abacus, 2000).

[62] Ibid.

King says that Jesus does not condemn this desire for recognition but explains how it is rightly conferred in the kingdom of God. "And so, Jesus gave us a new norm of greatness. If you want to be important—wonderful. If you want to be recognized—wonderful. If you want to be great—wonderful. But recognize that he who is greatest among you shall be your servant. (*Amen*) That's a new definition of greatness."[63] Being conscious of your consumption is necessary to have a **surplus**. Having a **surplus** is more important than being a drum major out in front. And distributing **surplus** to the disadvantaged, poor, and homeless is a magnificent way to be a great and righteous servant.

Here is the great economic lesson of Jesus on consumption. It is not about a specific number or amount. It is not a specific coefficient relative to production. It is not a specific portion of **surplus**. The right amount of consumption for a disciple of Jesus is the amount that sustains him or her and allows them to dedicate themselves to the tasks appropriate to their gifts.

If production is meager, sufficient consumption may reflect the discipline of John. If production is abundant, consumption may reflect the total variety and breadth of God's blessing. The concept of sharing and giving is central to Jesus's message. Paul reminds us in 1 Timothy 5:8, "Anyone who does not provide for their relatives, and especially for their own household, has denied the faith and is worse than an unbeliever."

That is why he states in 2 Timothy 2:6 "The hardworking farmer should be the first to receive a share of the crops."[64] Jesus himself knows he has work to do in order to complete his ministry. He will take the opportunity to feed himself during the Passover just before his passion and again on more than one occasion after his resurrection.

---

[63] Ibid.

[64] Radmacher, ed.

7
SURPLUS—THE DIFFERENCE BETWEEN PRODUCTION AND CONSUMPTION f(h)

Then he said, "This is what I'll do.
I will tear down my barns and build bigger ones,
and there I will store my **surplus** grain."

—Luke 12:18 (NIV)

Surplus is the consequence of the human function $f(h)$ (**production - consumption**). It could be called the net human function. Only a positive number insures the continued growth and flourishing of humanity. This chapter will examine it in more detail.

SURPLUS IN ECONOMICS AND THEOLOGY

Surplus is defined in modern English as an amount of something left over when requirements have been met. Its etymology goes back to its combined Latin roots of *super* (over, above) and *plus* (more). The modern definition of **surplus** is appropriate to our model, since it represents the positive difference between production and the requirement of consumption. We have discussed consumption in the context of the immediate food and water, which are requirements for sustaining human life. We labor to produce both food and water on a continuing basis for our primary needs.

Any amount of food or water that remains after we have supplied those requirements is a **surplus**. If we cannot produce enough food and water for our vital requirements, it is called a famine or a drought and without relief brings death relatively quickly. The amount of food and water produced to sustain human life is represented by the human function $f(h)$. If we only produce that amount of food and water, we live but cannot grow the population. It is the **surplus** of food and water over our immediate needs that provides for the healthy growth of humanity.

After Adam and Eve left the garden, producing a consistent **surplus** in all places at all times has proved impossible. Famine and drought have been the constant companions of humanity throughout history. Humans had to search for ways to carry their surpluses forward to sustain themselves during times of difficulty.

Barns and silos were invented to store grain for future consumption. Water was gathered into huge holding vessels called cisterns for future drinking. The greater the **surplus** of food and water, the more fortified the city. The more fortified the city, the more stable the society and its ability to sustain the division of labor to manifest ever greater art and culture.

SURPLUS IN ECONOMICS

By completing the model for the human function $f(h)$ where **production – consumption** = **surplus**, we have entered an area of firmer footing for the economist. So that they are not tempted to race ahead at this point in erroneous directions, we must provide some delimiting statements. **Surplus**, as used in this model, has no connection to the Marshallian concept of producer or consumer **surplus**, whereby an actor gains a monetary advantage if able to achieve a transaction at a price better than they would otherwise have been willing to supply or purchase.

To best understand what the scriptures have to tell us, we will remain within a strictly agrarian, distributive economy, such as was found in the early Levant. Concepts such as money (other than for barter), savings, investment, capital, and the like will have to wait until later chapters of the book. This very limited model of the human function $f(h)$ must be consistently adhered to if we are to communicate accurately.

SURPLUS IN THEOLOGY

Similarly, we must caution theologians that their jargon must also be delimited. We do not equate **surplus** to πλοῦτος (*ploutos*: riches), מִיסָכְנ (*nekes*: wealth), or μαμωνᾶς (*mamónas*: mammon). These concepts differ from **surplus** and only arise as derivatives of **surplus**. They only occur after decisions have been made about the **surplus** distribution.

Ploutos and *nekes* occur when the distributor designates **surplus** as the private property of a single individual and the amount of distribution is over and above what that person can reasonably consume themselves. Often, but not always, the distributor directs the **surplus** to themselves making themselves wealthy. If a person produces a **surplus** that they acknowledge is someone else's (Pharaoh's or God's, for instance), then they are not wealthy until they distribute to themselves a portion of that **surplus** that is more than they can reasonably consume.

This would be the case of the servants in the parable of talents or minas, church leaders, NGOs, foundation managers, and business organizations. *Mamónas* occurs when the distributor exchanges the short-term perishable **surplus** for a more durable item of future barter (money) such as gold or silver. These derivatives of **surplus** will be treated in the next chapter. The original biblical languages do not provide an etymological basis for the word **surplus**. The words closest to the concept are περίσσευμα (*perisseuma*: abundance) in Greek and בֹר (*robe*: abundance) in Hebrew.

These words are the primary words used in connection with food. There are, however, a number of other words variously translated as plentiful, prosperity, multitude, and others that are helpful in understanding biblical guidance under the model. Food—its production, consumption, and the storage of **surplus**—are important motifs in the Bible, and there is much instruction regarding them.

The Old Testament

The Old Testament, known to Jews as the *TANAKH*, is a self-revelation of God, who chooses to enter into a singular relationship with a particular people—Israel. The relationship is codified by express covenants or testaments.

Some theologians segment the first covenant into three periods: Creation to Noah, Noah to Abraham, and Abraham to Moses. Each period is concluded with a specific mutual obligation and specific sign—the rainbow, circumcision, and Sabbath.[65] For Christian theologians, the Sinai Covenant has come to symbolize the relationship between God and his people up to the arrival of Jesus, when the second or New Covenant is entered into. The Sinai Covenant, intermediated by Moses, is spelled out very specifically. As long as Israel remains true to God by not committing idolatry, keeping the Sabbath, reverencing his sanctuary, and obeying his commandments, then God will cause them to flourish by holding enemies and wild animals in abeyance, bringing peace, and providing for a continuous ***surplus*** *of food*. His explicit words in Leviticus 26 are as follows:

> [4] Then I will give you rain in its season, the land shall yield its produce, and the trees of the field shall yield their fruit. [5] Your threshing shall last till the time of vintage, and the vintage shall last till the time of sowing; you shall eat your bread to the full, and dwell in your land safely. [Later] [10] You shall eat the old harvest, and clear out the old because of the new.[66]

We can see that he expects them to preserve the **surplus** in silos and barns and draw from them on a FIFO (first in, first out) basis. Thus, the **surplus** was to have continuity and longevity supporting the human function $f(h)$. That is what would allow them to be fruitful and multiply. Prior to Moses such **surplus** was not continuously available and required the intercession of God to perpetuate his people. Such was the Joseph Novella.

There is no more straightforward explication of the human function $f(h)$ and the role of **surplus** than the Joseph novella found in Genesis 37–50. It is a story that seems to pit the need for food (the human function $f(h)$) against God's covenant with Abram to build a nation in the promised land. Not once but three times Abram is told by God that he will father many nations and his descendants will be given the land of Canaan as their promised land. God even changes his name to Abraham as a sign of the covenant. (Gen 12:1–3, 12:7, and 17:5)

But grazing and farming are challenging for the growing family on marginal land and they are able to just barely sustain themselves, i.e. $f(h) = 0$.

---

[65] Bruce M. Metzger, ed. *The Oxford Companion to the Bible*, ed. Michael D. Coogan (New York: Oxford University Press, 1993), 84.
[66] NKJV.

When famine strikes the land, Abraham seeks to resettle in Egypt, where the Nile River insures food. But God does not want Abraham to build a nation in Egypt and sends him back to Canaan. His sons, Isaac and Jacob, continue to live in Canaan and grow the γενεά (family).

But the land remains a challenge and requires an extraordinarily gifted economic manager to fulfill God's covenant to Abraham. God sends Joseph, a gloriously imbued administrator, to manage the economic household of Jacob in the challenging land of Canaan so that the οἶκος (household) might prosper. But instead of accepting God's gift, the sons of Jacob rebel against God almost causing the extinction of the Jewish people. But God's plan, though it may be diverted by the actions of men, will ultimately succeed. How God uses the bad actions of men for good and the continuation of his plan is the novella of Joseph. (Gen. 37–50)

Through an extraordinary sequence of events, which we will not recount here, Pharaoh installs Joseph as his second-in-command. The second-in-command in all administrative matters in ancient Egypt was the Grand Vizier, also called the "Overseer of the Royal Estates." The economy of ancient Egypt is described as "distributive" and for thousands of years it "treated private property as stipulative and merely conditional, and the market as subordinate and subject to close political supervision."[67]

"A further mark of the distributive economy ... [was] that transactions are made in commodities of real value, that is, barter, and not of symbolic value, that is, money."[68] The authority of the Egyptian distributive market was Pharaoh or his delegated person. That person's authority was publically visible through his trappings and accouterments. Therefore, Joseph was dressed in fine linen with a gold chain around his neck. On his finger was placed the Pharaoh's signet ring that he would use to affix Pharaoh's symbol to the new decrees.

For the next seven years of plenty, Joseph discouraged grain exports and excess consumption by decreeing a forced savings of 20 percent of all crops grown. The grain was efficiently husbanded under the sole authority of Pharaoh and within the protection of the walled cities until the amount was so great that it could no longer be tallied.

After seven years, a scorching wind came from the East (Gen. 41:6 NKJV), the desert wind known in North Africa as the *hamsin*, and the Nile

---

[67] Neusner, 8.

[68] Ibid., 7.

began to recede. Crop yields greatly diminished and the Egyptians turned to Pharaoh for bread. "Then Pharaoh said to all the Egyptians, 'Go to Joseph' whatever he says to you, do" (Gen. 41:55 NIV).

Joseph set up a grain market for the Egyptians, which was neither eleemosynary nor unfair. He sold them grain at the same price that they had sold to merchant traders when grain was plentiful. This was not a market economy, which would have demanded a higher price (even gouging) during periods of extreme demand and monopolized supply. In distributive economics, money serves as a medium of barter and bears only intrinsic value, as do the goods for which it is exchanged. The price for Egypt's grain was known and had been the same for thousands of years.

A **surplus** was the means necessary for the stability and maintenance of the land and therefore limited by its ends. So, during periods of plenty in Egypt, the excess grain was bartered, directly or indirectly, for more land, cattle, horses, and labor. The labor would have come in the form of more family or as in the case of Joseph more slaves. Once future factors of production were acquired, they would accumulate silver to better store value for future unforeseen needs.

Now experiencing the increasing famine, the Egyptians voluntarily traded their silver for grain. As the years went by and the famine intensified they would trade the factors of farming they had acquired for grain over the years with Midianite merchants. First the livestock was traded. Finally, the land was bartered with the right to remain on it in exchange for rent in the form of crop participation.

Joseph's prescience in accumulating the grain was now matched by his brilliance in amalgamating its ownership under Pharaoh. What he did was concentrate the means of production in the hands of Pharaoh. He single-handedly transformed the structure of the treasury inflows from a time-to-time detestable tax to a continuous rent with the goodwill of saving the nation from starvation.

For as Joseph said to them, "You meant evil against me, but God meant it for good, in order to bring it about as it is this day, to save many people alive."[69] A number of years later, Joseph said, "I am about to die. But God will surely come to your aid and take you up out of this land to the land he promised on oath to Abraham, Isaac and Jacob."[70] It would be for Moses, much later, to

---

[69] Barker, ed., Genesis 50:20.
[70] Radmacher, ed., Genesis 50:24.

continue the Abrahamic covenant by taking a much larger tribe of Hebrews out of Egypt to the promised land.

This scriptural pericope tells us that God will provide exogenous factors to us, if necessary, when we struggle with $f(h)$ in order to fulfill his plan. This pericope also tells us about a gift—the Joseph gift. It is the ability to create and manage **surplus** even in challenging times. Not everyone has that gift. Starting a company is hard—statistically most startups fail.

But some are led by people with an entrepreneurial spirit, tenacity, and great insight. They, too, have the Joseph gift. These people develop products that allow humankind to not only exist but to flourish. They create jobs that people with different gifts can thrive on. People with the Joseph gift are important in building up the body of Christ and funding its missional objectives.

The New Testament

Jesus is our model in all things, including **surplus**. During Jesus's mission on Earth, he got involved personally a number of times to create food and drink. Famously, he made the best tasting wine of the evening for a wedding party. Even more demonstrably, he is chronicled as personally feeding thousands and thousands of people. He identified himself with the human function $f(h)$ and the people's need to drink and eat. But beyond that, he demonstrates the divine affiliation with **surplus**.

Mark 8:1–10 and Matthew 15:32–39 tell the same story of how he miraculously created food to feed the multitudes.

In both accounts, it says that the people ate and ἐχορτάσθησαν (*echortasthēsan*: were satisfied). Jesus supported the human function $f(h)$. The excess of the human function $f(h)$ is what our model deems **surplus**. Mark and Matthew both report substantial excesses. The excesses gathered up in the seven baskets were not scraps but fragments—more pieces of food.[71] One might conclude that the people took the excess food with them to share and demonstrate to others the story they had just witnessed. The **surplus** would have "grown" the story beyond just its participants and thus achieved its importance, so that more than one gospel writer recounted it.

Again, in John 21, after a full day of futile effort, Peter casts his net one last time into the water at Jesus's command. Jesus personally creates a

---

[71] Bruner, 561.

surplus of fish in a single throw of Peter's net. We know it is a **surplus** because Peter has to drag the net to the shore to insure it does not rip. The net isn't designed for this big a haul!

Jesus confirms the human function $f(h)$ by producing food and drink for people to consume. But beyond that, he labors to create a **surplus**. I believe that is the model he wants us to emulate as we produce—we should always aim for a **surplus**.

WHAT IS WEALTH AND WHO ARE THE WEALTHY?

We have already defined **surplus** as the difference between production and consumption. Is wealth the same thing as **surplus**? Not exactly. We define wealth as a subset of **surplus**. Wealth is that portion of the **surplus** that is specifically set aside by the manager for his or her own future consumption. In Jesus's time, **surplus** and wealth were generally conflated. Stored food and things to barter for future food, including gold, were the major portion of wealth.

But it also included the factors of production—land, seed, and labor. Land ownership was relegated to a very small percentage of the population. Jesus's teachings extended beyond such a narrow group. While it would include those with extensive land holdings (the rich young ruler), it would also include those with large amounts of food and money (Zacchaeus) right down to a person with a mite or two cloaks.

Money was the major symbol of wealth. Not everyone had coins. Most people had to acquire specific coins for tax and tithing purposes. People understood that the charity of the Good Samaritan came from coins to buy food and shelter. They would have felt it strange for the Good Samaritan to have signed over his family's farm. The land was known as the inheritance, something to be passed on to the next generation. Only in extremis, such as the last days of the Jerusalem church, would assets such as land be consumed.

This is important because, in the capitalist economy, money is fungible. Fungible has nothing to do with an organism but simply means mutual interchangeability. Thus, money in a personal checking account can represent today's meal, a payment on the house mortgage, or support for a student at school. It can also represent savings in excess of those obligations. The balance at any one time is not necessarily an indicator of wealth.

Wealth would be the residual, discretionary balance—or savings. Relatively few people today own farms. So where do they put that portion of **surplus** (savings) intended for increased future productivity? Stocks and bonds represent investments in corporations that produce not only today's food, but also products that will increase productivity and therefore greater amounts of food in the future.

Future increased productivity is required for a greater population and hopefully the byproduct of additional **surplus**. This is the basis for the virtuous cycle of the capitalist system.

MANAGING THE **SURPLUS**—THE WEALTHY

We have seen both in Old Testament and New Testament testimony that whenever God or Jesus was the producer, there was a **surplus**. Whether it was the fruit in the Garden of Eden or the catching of fish, divine production always provided more food than was required for those who were hungry. This is of great comfort to those who hunger and thirst, for they have been assured that there are no shortages in heaven. God will both produce and distribute. It is critical to note that God and Jesus primarily distributed **surplus** to others. But what about "thy kingdom come here on earth as it is in heaven?" What role do the disciples of Christ have to play in offsetting want with **surplus** here on earth?

We already know that the human function **f(h)** must produce a **surplus** if humanity is to flourish. But as the economist Thomas Malthus pointed out, just a minimal **surplus** will not be sufficient in the face of hardship—famine and drought. The productive application of reinvesting **surplus** to grow an ever-increasing amount of food is required.

As we have seen from the Joseph novella, Joseph's brothers did not have the gift to apply **surplus** for the purpose of growing more food. But Pharaoh saw that Joseph did have a divine gift and put him in charge of creating and distributing **surplus**. Joseph was given authority over **surplus** second only to Pharaoh.

People are powerful who have the absolute authority over how **surplus** is distributed. Power accrues to those who have that authority. The larger the **surplus** at their discretion, the more people they can impact with its distribution. The more people they can impact, the more powerful they become over those people.

There is an absolute correlation between being wealthy and being powerful. People tend to favor themselves in that distribution. They tend to retain more than they can reasonably consume, thereby setting by a personal

surplus. Is that personal **surplus** a demonstration of prudence against unanticipated personal difficulties or a signal of moral failure? That question goes beyond the economic relationships of the exegetical economic model, because it speaks to the motivation and intentions of the actors. And that is the heart of the wealth teachings that we will turn to later in this book. It is the motivations of the wealthy, what is in their hearts, that concerns Jesus. And he speaks to that issue on many occasions, which we will review.

But simply being in charge of the distribution of food made Joseph powerful, not evil. Likewise, to be in charge of any distribution of **surplus** can make one wealthy but not necessarily evil. In fact, the responsibility of being wealthy and managing the **surplus** to support God's purpose was a crucial gift. Ecclesiastes 5:19 tells us, "As for every man to whom God has given riches and wealth, and given him power to eat of it, to receive his heritage and rejoice in his labor—this is the gift of God."[72]

Abraham, Isaac, Jacob, Joseph, and Moses were all in charge of great surpluses and must be labeled wealthy. And yet, they were all blessed. Their wisdom in its distribution was essential to the fulfilling of the Abrahamic Covenant.

In the New Testament, we find the Greek word πλούσιος (*plousios*: rich, abounding in, wealthy) to describe a person who has a **surplus** (abundance) over which he has personal discretion. The word πλούσιος is attached to Joseph of Arimathea and Zacchaeus. Both of these men had a personal relationship with Jesus and played important positive roles in his ministry. Πλούσιος is even attached to Jesus himself only to make the point that he rejected it as not radical enough to get people's attention.

Jesus did not reject being wealthy because it was evil but because his power would be more demonstrable without it. Paradoxically, he was poor and yet a great distributor of **surplus** to others. As a poor, peripatetic rabbi or as an all-powerful and wealthy God—the Trinity is good. The obedient disciple Paul puts a fine point on it. In Philippians 4:11–13, he states that a disciple of Christ can operate in want or περισσεύειν ἐν παντὶ (in a **surplus** of everything). But in either case, their "strength to do all things comes from Christ."

Paul is confirming that there should be no derogatory attribution to any disciples simply because they have an abundance or **surplus** that they control or oversee. Jesus makes the same point when he stays at the house of

---

[72] Radmacher, ed.

Zacchaeus in Jericho. He says in Luke 19:9, "Today salvation has come to this house."

This was his response when he heard that Zacchaeus was going to distribute a substantial part of his **surplus** to the poor and those he may have wronged. How Zacchaeus managed and distributed his **surplus**, not the **surplus** itself, determined his blessing from God. But the manner in which he had previously managed his **surplus** (retained it for himself) had caused Jesus to describe him as "lost." We now turn to the quintessential quandary of the πλούσιος (wealthy). What are the motivations that lie in the hearts of the wealthy that cause them to be "saved" or "lost"?

Managing the **surplus** means making the decisions of what amount of the **surplus** will go for consumption, what will be retained to protect for future consumption, how much will be reinvested to increase future productivity, and what will be disbursed in charity. Individuals, company CEOs, and ecclesiastical leaders share this common responsibility. If they manage their own **surplus**, we call them wealthy; if they manage other people's **surplus**, we call them stewards. They all accrue power based on their roles of distribution. That authority alone—to retain, reinvest, or disburse the **surplus**—is sufficient to manifest power.

8
PLUTOGENICS—THE WEALTH DISEASE

You say, "I am rich;
I have acquired wealth and do not need a thing."
But you do not realize that you are
wretched, pitiful, poor, blind and naked.

—Revelation 3:17 (NIV)

Why are money and wealth spoken about so pejoratively in the Bible? It is not that they are evil in and of themselves. But they can be carriers of disease for those that come into contact with them. In this chapter, we will examine that disease. Who does it affect? What are the symptoms? What are the consequences of the unchecked disease? What is the cure?

Jesus talks extensively about the wealthy in his teachings. Who is he addressing? Is it the 1 percenters, the 10 percenters, or simply people who manage a **surplus**? Is he talking to me? What is he saying? These are the questions we will attempt to address here.

For Jesus, wealthy is not a comparative term. He does not talk of the super-rich differently than simply the rich. Jesus does not give us an "out" if we can identify someone richer than we are. The terms rich or wealthy simply refer to someone who manages **surplus**—no matter its size.

The distribution of **surplus** has the power to guide people's actions by paying them, feeding them, or even bribing them. So, there is a correlation between the size of **surplus** managed and the amount of concomitant power.

And power is a toxin to the soul. The more power one possesses, the more caustic the environment to their spiritual well-being.

A young person can idealistically enter a profession for the betterment of the world, only to find, as in Mark 8:36, that—as they achieved more and more financial success—they became a person they didn't wish to be. Why?

Thus far, we have been fleshing out an economic model that reflects how God intends the world to operate on its grandest scale. You will recall that exegetical economics is defined as *the interaction of humankind with the creation and each other for the purpose of growing and sustaining itself.* Our model demonstrates that humankind only grows and flourishes in a state of **surplus**. Further we observed that the men and women who direct the distribution and allocation of surpluses have power and are deemed "wealthy."

Now we want to move from the impersonal designation of "wealthy" contained in our conceptual model to a more specific understanding of who fits that description. We want to start talking about real people and their motivations. That is how we come to understand the relevance of Jesus's teachings to ourselves. We have to start talking about motivations and then look inside ourselves where only God and we can see.

In the time of Jesus, the hierarchical, distributive agrarian economy made certain groups wealthy. Certainly, high Roman officials up to and including Caesar, who were the beneficiaries of the tribute collected from their empire were wealthy. Secondly, the Herodian dynasty that ruled the people and collected their own taxes were wealthy. Tax collectors who exacted the taxes from the people were wealthy. The high priest and his circle that benefited from the various offerings made through the Temple system were wealthy.

Some landowners were wealthy. Agrarian concentration had been going on for some time and had acquired the appellation *latifundia* (Latin: *lātus*, "spacious" + *fundus*, "farm, estate"). Such large estates were supported by slave labor if Roman, or peasants and servants if Jewish, which allowed their owners to generate **surplus** and become wealthy. All of these ancient people had distribution authority over large surpluses and fit our model's definition of wealthy. Jesus used all of the wealthy people of his time, no matter how they acquired their wealth, for learning examples and teachable moments.

Most job descriptions have changed since the time of Jesus. But there is more **surplus** than ever before and more people in charge of its distribution than ever in history. However, the corrosive effect of being in charge of the distribution of **surplus** has not changed at all. **Surplus** distribution gives people power over the lives of others. The more people that are affected by that distribution, the more power the distributor (wealthy person) has.

Certainly, this includes politicians at all levels who form budgets that are collectively in the trillions of dollars. It includes pastors of large churches (including the pope), who deal with budgets in the millions and billions of dollars. It includes CEOs of large corporations and presidents of major universities who make **surplus** allocation decisions among thousands of employees, students, and stockholders.

Some will claim that they are but the agents of stakeholders in their organization and not really the owner. But power is the litmus test. If they have the power of distribution, then they are wealthy, according to our model.

But if we are not counted among these, are we wealthy? If we are not outside the chain of command in an organization, are we excluded? We have to look to our personal **surplus** to answer that question. Will even a modest distribution of our personal **surplus** feed a large group of people for a long time? Will our excess clothes protect those in need? Can we afford to contribute to erect shelters for those in need?

John the Baptist famously included almost everyone saying in Luke 3:11, "He who has two tunics, let him give to him who has none; and he who has food, let him do likewise." Jesus, watching a widow donate two mites to the church, said in Luke 21: 3–4, "Truly I say to you that this poor widow has put in more than all; for all these out of their abundance have put in offerings for God, but she out of her poverty put in all the livelihood that she had."[73]

John and Jesus do not establish a minimum **surplus** before their teachings apply. In fact, the smaller the **surplus** the greater the blessing in its distribution (just the opposite of the greater corrosive power of a larger **surplus**). One purpose of these great teachings is to convict those of us who have more than two shirts or two pennies that we should be much more generous in our giving to those in need.

In business, when raising money for a new venture, there is an expectation that the amount of investment will be returned along with additional payment for the risk. When the risk/reward is great it is advisable to share the risk with other people. That way if the venture is not successful, you remain viable to try again. But it doesn't work that way in raising money for charitable purposes. A charity means there is no expected return of the donation. As with an investment, the promoter of the charity should demonstrate their

---

[73] Ibid.

commitment by putting in the first dollars. People are never more inclined to contribute to a cause than when they see a pastor moved to write the first check. Giving is a spiritually healthy act for the manager of any size **surplus** as well as the charity promoter.

The unchurched wealthy are a tough audience to reach. They are laser-focused on making more **surplus**. They are gifted at it. It is reinforcing and addictive. At such a point, their soul is no longer part of their life. As Tolstoy observed, "Materialists mistake that which limits life, for life itself."[74] They spend so much time in the office, or the casino, that they do not experience the joy which comes with the soul's experiencing the love of God through others. Cold hard logic is sometimes the icebreaker.

Blaine Pascal (1623–1662), a wealthy man himself, used the simile of a wager to get their attention. He appealed to their brain, hoping that he would ultimately connect with their heart. Pascal was a successful entrepreneur who tried to connect God with businesspeople. He invented the first mechanical adding machine. It was a very expensive machine and only the governmental tax office could afford it.

> Pascal argues that, given the terms of the Wager, it is not simply prudent, it is practically obligatory to bet on God's existence and illogical and utterly foolish to bet against Him. For consider: if you bet on His existence, you stand to win an infinite reward (an eternity in paradise) at the risk of only a small loss (whatever earthly pleasures you would be required to forgo during your mortal life). On the other hand, if you bet against His existence, you risk the possibility of an infinite loss (loss of paradise—along with the possibility of an eternity in Hell) for only a limited gain (the opportunity to enjoy a few years' worth of worldly delights).[75]

Some would go further and state the foregone "worldly delights" were simply excesses which were harmful to you in this world as well.

Jesus also studied the secular wealthy and remarked in Luke 16 how shrewd they were in worldly business as opposed to the "sons of light." He said Christians could learn something from this. In verse 9, he says, "I tell

---

[74] Leo Tolstoy, *Essays and Letters* (London: Grant Richards, 1903), 367.
[75] "Blaise Pascal (1623–1662)," http://www.iep.utm.edu/pascal-b/#SSH2bv.

you, use worldly wealth to gain friends for yourselves, so that when it is gone, you will be welcomed into eternal dwellings." The friends he speaks of are outside of their normal circle—they are the poor, disadvantaged, and needy. Jim Elliot, a missionary who gave his life for the faith in Ecuador in 1956, caught the true essence of Jesus's meaning. He said, "He is no fool who parts with that which he cannot keep, when he is sure to be recompensed with that which he cannot lose."[76] Non-Christian people who create **surplus** are not fools and are very logical. The arguments of Tolstoy, Pascal, and Elliot can reach them in a special way.

While a lost wealthy person may be distracted and hard to reach, their salvation can be a multiplication opportunity to help so many other lives through the **surplus** that they manage. There are many biblical and contemporary wealthy people who manage their **surplus** in consonance with God's loving instruction. God intends for both the manager of the **surplus** distribution and the beneficiaries of that distribution to be in community together and share great blessings. But there are many with diseased hearts that may already be writing checks to charity and putting their names on hospitals. How do we identify those we can help, who are staring at the "eye of the needle?"[77]

Checks, like works, are not immunization against the disease of wealth. The souls of the wealthy remain extremely vulnerable to the disease and are easily attacked. It causes the wealthy to live as slaves to mammon, separate themselves from community, and die without God. The tragedy is that this is not God's intention for the managers of **surplus**.

I call this disease *plutogenics*. Effective treatment for any disease begins with an accurate diagnosis. What are the symptoms of this disease which primarily infects the wealthy? Eugene Peterson's encounter with a similar rare but deadly disease will help us. Eugene H. Peterson is professor emeritus of spiritual theology at Regent College, Vancouver, British Columbia. Peterson was a theologian and a philologist. The outcome of his passion is a contemporary translation of the Bible entitled *The Message*.

Peterson is a "mirror" user and points to himself for teaching purposes. He talks of going to the hospital for one problem only to contract a much more serious disease. What he experienced was described by his doctor as

---

[76] Elisabeth Elliot, *Shadow of the Almighty: The Life & Testament of Jim Elliot* (New York: Harper, 1958), 108.
[77] Radmacher, ed., Matthew 19:24.

"iatrogenic," meaning a disease caught in the process of healing. Much later, he learned that this was so prevalent in hospitals nationwide, that it presented a very significant threat to the health of the country.

His syncretic mind immediately turned to another place that people go to for healing—the church. That same church brings us to salvation through Jesus Christ, baptism, and a nurturing community led by the Holy Spirit. But there are diseases lurking there that are only available to churchgoers. Always the wordsmith, he coined the term "eusebeigenic," which means a sin committed in the act of trying to be righteous. It has a paradoxical appeal. It is an unconscious step backward in the life of someone who is trying to move forward and be successful.[78]

For reasons similar to Peterson's, I named the wealth disease—*Plutogenics*. It is a combination word from the Greek πλούσιος (*plousios*: rich) and γένος (*genos*: kind). Like *eusebeigenic*, it has a paradoxical connotation. It is a disease primarily affecting those who are gifted enough to succeed financially and build **surplus**. Their success achieves the very **surplus** needed for human flourishing. But it also brings corrupting power.

Augustine notes, "Evil is not a substance but is rather the corruption or misuse of what is by nature good."[79] *Plutogenics* is a disease that hides in the heart and cannot be detected by an MRI or CAT scan. It has, however, been diagnosed for thousands of years because the Bible provides its symptoms and the way they manifest. We will now look at how the Bible describes the symptoms of this deadly disease.

THE SYMPTOM—ΠΛΕΟΝΕΞΙΑ (*PLEONEXIA*: COVETOUSNESS, AVARICE, AGGRESSION, DESIRE FOR ADVANTAGE)

This symptom manifests when wealth may only be incipient. We do not know the wealth situation of the person in Luke 12:13–15 who calls on Jesus to provide support for his inheritance. The man is looking for an advantage in dealing with his brother. Jesus uses the opportunity not only to deny involvement in such an endeavor but to caution against all such

---

[78] Eugene H. Peterson, *Tell It Slant: A Conversation on the Language of Jesus in His Stories and Prayers* (Cambridge: Wm B. Eerdmans Publishing Co, 2008), 88.

[79] Justo L. González, *Faith and Wealth : A History of Early Christian Ideas on the Origin, Significance, and Use of Money*, 1st ed. (San Francisco: Harper & Row, 1990), 214.

kinds of covetousness. A number of examples are also laid out in the tenth commandment, which covers just about everything that belongs to your neighbor (someone else). The Hebrew word in Exodus 20:17 is חָמַד (*chamad*: to desire, take pleasure in).

Interestingly, all the objects referred to in that commandment have an economic value and reflect **surplus**, with perhaps the exception of the spouse, which is sexual. Jesus's admonitions are stark when referring to **surplus** of food and money. The heart of his concern is that the individual's greed for **surplus** goes beyond his need for consumption. It initiates a downward spiral to build an ever-increasing **surplus** for its own sake.

Jesus painted a vivid picture in Luke 12:16, saying, "The ground of a certain rich man yielded plentifully. And he thought within himself, saying, 'What shall I do, since I have no room to store my crops?' So, he said, 'I will do this: I will pull down my barns and build greater, and there I will store all my crops and my goods.'"

Covetousness is a black-hole trait. It will never be satiated. There is never enough. As Ecclesiastes 5:10 tells us, "Whoever loves money never has enough; whoever loves wealth is never satisfied with their income. This too is meaningless." This lust can be driven by competition, not fear of the future. We may have an automobile that meets all of our travel needs, but does our neighbor have a more expensive one? In advanced cases, such as the extremely wealthy, you could substitute second home, airplane, boat, jewelry, etc. The more prominent the display of their possessions, the more obvious the disease is to others and the more invisible the disease is to themselves. This disease is extremely hard to cure in its advanced stages. The size of the yacht, including helipad, can be incredible.

The goal of *Forbes* magazine's fifth richest person in the world is not to become the sixth richest in the subsequent year. But the focus on a ranking can work against anyone. Once you take your eye off of the gift God gave you and focus only on the money, you will fall prey to Proverbs 23:5: "When you set your eyes on it, it is gone. For wealth certainly makes itself wings, like an eagle that flies toward the heavens. The greedy are constantly returning to the thought of numbers and their minds do not dwell on God."

The truth of Matthew 6:24 becomes clear and undeniable. "No one can serve two masters. Either you will hate the one and love the other, or you will be devoted to the one and despise the other. You cannot serve both God and money." The greedy have lost touch with their gift that built the **surplus**. They are about making money for money's sake.

They have made money their idol. Idolatry, εἰδωλολατρεία (*eidólolatria*: worship or service of an image), for the wealthy is much more likely to be a bank account than a golden calf, but it is equally deadly for their souls. The relationship of **surplus** to greed is much like the relationship of faith to works. It depends on the origin of our motivation. Are we saved by works? No. We are saved by grace through faith. But a strong faith will leave works in its path. If we have a gift from God that others value, then practicing that gift will leave **surplus** in its path. We need not be driven by greed to generate **surplus**.

How does greed differ from building **surplus**? Our exegetical model for the human function $f(h)$ showed **surplus** as a necessary requirement for the sustenance of all humankind. If that is part of God's plan, then it must be possible for people to generate **surplus** and maintain a healthy soul. A paraphrase of Romans 12:2 might say the righteous are not conformed to the world but build **surplus**, which is good in the eyes of God because the focus of their minds is on their gifts.

When entrepreneurs get excited, it is about seeing a solution to problems that they can solve more cost effectively than anyone else. They will solve the problem by increasing efficiency or productivity. If someone starts a company that becomes valuable because it has developed a food source that thrives in areas that are arid and difficult to cultivate, then the increased value of their ownership of that company did not come at the expense of another.

In fact, by creating more food, they reflect the very goal of the human function $f(h)$, while at the same time being rewarded for their ingenuity. Another example would be compensation raises received by employees of a company. Their supervisors have determined that their productivity in the firm has increased, and they are rewarded for that. Neither of these examples demonstrates greed, because the rewards involved increased productivity and were given by third-party supervisors or investors. This too is biblical, as Proverbs 27:2 notes:

"Let someone else praise you, and not your own mouth; an outsider, and not your own lips."

THE SYMPTOM—ΦΑΓΟΣ (*PHAGOS*: A GLUTTON), ΟἸΝΟΠΟΤΗΣ (*OINOPOTÉS*: A DRUNKARD)

These two words, especially in combination, describe a symptom of the wealth disease. In the time of Jesus, only people of means could afford more food and wine than they should eat or drink. For many years in the eighteenth century, gout was known as the rich man's disease. It is a form of arthritis that can be inflamed by excessive uric acid. The buildup of uric acid in the blood can be caused by excessive meat or beer in the diet—the kind of excessive diet that only a rich person could afford.

Since the time of Solomon, the idea of eating or drinking too much was known to be detrimental to your health and quality of life. Proverbs 23:20–21 notes, "Do not join those who drink too much wine or gorge themselves on meat, for drunkards and gluttons become poor, and drowsiness clothes them in rags."

Even without knowing the exact physiological consequences, they recognized that a huge meal would make you sleepy and sap your productivity. Nothing about that has changed much in the last three thousand or so years! Drunkenness is not now exclusive to the wealthy, but it is easier for them.

Wealthy people cannot only afford strong spirits, but they have more discretionary time and can hide in large houses away from judgmental eyes. Excess drinking lowers inhibitions, as 1 Corinthians 10:7 cautions: "Do not be idolaters, as some of them were; as it is written: 'The people sat down to eat and drink and got up to indulge in revelry.'"

When the Pharisees wanted to strike Jesus hard in Matthew 11:19, they accused him of being "a glutton and a drunkard, a friend of tax collectors and sinners." But as Jesus said, "Wisdom is proved right by her deeds." His actions to heal and save so many proved them wrong. He struck the golden mean. He taught us to pray for a specific amount of bread that would be sufficient for the day.

This translation of ἐπιούσιος (*epiousios*: for the morrow, necessary, sufficient) in the Lord's Prayer of Matthew 6:11 gives us a sense of portion. The Roman soldier of that day was given one and a half to two pounds of bread while on the march.[80] This amount would allow the soldier to maintain his strength for the day. Eating only our portion daily gives us strength for a lifetime.

While some feel that modern gluttony can devolve to eating delicacies, I find old-fashion excess still rampant today. Not only are hot dog-eating contests uncomfortable to watch, but the food is amassed and disgorged while many in the world are still hungry. Personally, I find "all you can eat"

---

[80] Robert Cowley, Geoffrey Parker, and Society for Military History (U.S.), *The Reader's Companion to Military History* (Boston: Houghton Mifflin, 1996), 161.

buffets and prepaid meals extremely sinister in their temptations. I lose the fact that I am consuming more food than is healthy while trying to stay cost-effective. Paradoxically, smaller portions of food with greater preparation, and therefore more expense (within reason), seem better to me both physically and spiritually.

After all, we know that Jesus produced a higher quality of wine when he supplied it for the wedding feast at his mother's request, in his first miracle.[81] But C. S. Lewis makes a good point when he says, "But what do quantities matter, provided we can use a human belly and palate to produce querulousness, impatience, uncharitableness and self-concern?"[82] He seems to be channeling Paul, who says in Philippians 3:19, "Their destiny is destruction, their god is their stomach, and their glory is in their shame. Their mind is set on earthly things."

Food should be blessed for our use rather than worshipped as our focus. I think many of the wealthy eat proportionately well, but is their focus on the menu and variety rivaling their time and attention to God? Do they thank God for its provision? How do they treat the service providers waiting on them? Are they petulant, over-demanding, and never satisfied with the service and the meal? These are all food-eating distortions included in the concept of gluttony. Remembering that our bodies are temples into which we invite Christ should motivate us to eat and drink appropriately to keep them healthy.

THE SYMPTOM—ὙΠΕΡΗΦΑΝΟΣ (*HUPEREPHANOS*: PROUD, ARROGANT, DISDAINFUL)

Arrogance is a symptom of *plutogenics* that causes us to believe we are more important than someone else. We are all born equal in the eyes of God and yet given different individual gifts. Developing those gifts in music, sports or business can bring large amounts of **surplus** into our lives. Managing that **surplus** makes us "wealthy."

The caution here is pointed out in Galatians 6:4, which says, "Each one should test their own actions. Then they can take pride in themselves alone, without comparing themselves to someone else." But acquiring **surplus**

---

[81] John 2:1–11.

[82] C. S. Lewis, *The Complete C. S. Lewis Signature Classics*, 1st ed. (San Francisco: HarperSanFrancisco, 2002), Screwtape Letters XVII.

makes many do the opposite. They don't acknowledge the role God has played in their success. They don't hear Jeremiah's warning in 9:23, "Let not the wise boast of their wisdom or the strong boast of their strength or the rich boast of their riches."

The Lord repeatedly says—in Isaiah 2:12, Isaiah 23:9, Proverbs 8:13, Proverbs 16:5, and many other places—that the arrogant will fall because he will personally see to it. They will stumble and fall because they are so taken with themselves, they have left no room for God. Psalm 10:4 adds, "In his pride the wicked man does not seek him; in all his thoughts there is no room for God."

Celebrities are people whose very lives are branded, marketed, watched, and emulated. They set fashion and their every move is monitored by their Twitter following and the gossip press. They are constantly interviewed for their opinions and thoughts. Many use their celebrity platform to tell others how their lives should be governed.

But they are only human, and the press devours them as well as builds them up. Their tragedies, divorces, car crashes, drug overdoses, and aging are grist for the tabloid press. Proverbs 21:4 says, "Haughty eyes and a proud heart—the unplowed field of the wicked—produce sin." They have a public persona that does not reflect the feelings they have inside. Some try to make that persona their life by boasting they "did it my way."

First Timothy 6:7 points out the reality: "For we have brought nothing into the world, so we cannot take anything out of it either"—this includes the persona. Such a life will have exaggerated highs and lows. Tragically, some lows bring a self-inflicted end. But the real tragedy for public personalities is pointed out by all three synoptic gospel writers, in Matthew 10:32–33, Mark 8:38, and Luke 12:8–9. Those who do not publicly acknowledge Jesus in this life will be denied by him before God in eternity.

THE SYMPTOM—ΘΗΣΑΥΡΙΖΩ (*THÉSAURIZÓ*: I STORE UP, TREASURE UP, SAVE, LAY UP)

Wealthy people are those in charge of distributing **surplus**. When they distribute it all among themselves, it is called hoarding. Hoarding is the inability to share with others and a very distressing symptom of *plutogenics*. Ecclesiastes 5:13 says, "There is a grievous evil which I have seen under the sun: riches being hoarded by their owner to his hurt." It is so destructive that Jesus devoted a whole parable to it in Luke 12:

¹⁶ And he told them this parable: "The ground of a certain rich man yielded an abundant harvest. ¹⁷ He thought to himself, 'What shall I do? I have no place to store my crops.'

¹⁸ "Then he said, 'This is what I'll do. I will tear down my barns and build bigger ones, and there I will store my **surplus** grain. ¹⁹ And I'll say to myself, "You have plenty of grain laid up for many years. Take life easy; eat, drink and be merry."'

²⁰ "But God said to him, 'You fool! This very night your life will be demanded from you. Then who will get what you have prepared for yourself?'

²¹ "This is how it will be with whoever stores up things for themselves but is not rich toward God."

Hoarding does not always have the expected outcome. It is driven by fear and meant to insulate from unknown setbacks. The idea is that, by not sharing with others, one preserves more for himself. And yet Proverbs 11:24 states the reality that "one person gives freely, yet gains even more; another withholds unduly, but comes to poverty." In his letter, James seems almost to scream at the insanity of exploiting others to build a hoard for oneself in the face of an eschatological world and the return of Jesus. He points out that the cries of the oppressed are heard, the hoard is worthless, and all that they have hoarded condemns them at the hour of judgment.[83]

We may not feel the Parousia as intensely as James, but there must always be a concern for others by the wealthy in their distribution activities. Widows, orphans, and others, whomever is marginalized by society, are good choices for that distribution.

There will be a day of reckoning (although we don't know when), and Jesus will look to see who fed the hungry, gave water to the thirsty, and clothed the naked. As he said in Matthew 25:40, "Truly I tell you, whatever you did for one of the least of these brothers and sisters of mine, you did for me." What a great opportunity to serve the Lord! This is what storing up treasure in heaven is all about. Matthew 6:19 warns about earthly security, saying, "Do not store up for yourselves treasures on earth, where moth and rust destroy, and where thieves break in and steal."

One of the greatest financial planning worries of this generation is whether

---

[83] James 5:1–6.

they will outlive their means. To help in that endeavor Congress passed laws setting up individual retirement accounts. Such accounts—newer Roth legislation has made some improvements—provide for the compounding of earnings on a tax-free basis until they are ultimately distributed. Financial planners know the power of tax-free compounding and encourage clients to open such accounts at the earliest age possible and make the maximum contributions possible. Time is the key when even modest contributions can reach millions of dollars if compounded long enough. But Jesus is the greatest financial planner of all. In Matthew 19:21 and Luke 12:33, he exhorts all of us to make contributions to a heavenly IRA by giving to the poor and needy. He guarantees that it will compound and last us for an eternity—no matter the size of the contribution. He says, in Luke 12:34, if you make this investment, your heart cannot help but follow. What a deal—an investment that compounds to our eternal benefit and helps our hearts and souls in the here and now.

THE SYMPTOM—אָמֵט (*TAME*: UNCLEAN)

We normally don't associate wealth with the symptom of being unclean. But wealth can make us unclean in our hearts. It causes the sufferer to impose exile on himself. To be unclean is a Biblical designation for people who must be separated from the community. It stems from a health safety issue. There are many reasons to take such action. Leviticus 7:20 describes one situation: "But if anyone who is unclean eats any meat of the fellowship offering belonging to the LORD, THEY MUST BE CUT OFF FROM THEIR PEOPLE."

The Jewish oral and written tradition taught boundaries. Boundaries of ethnicity, boundaries of food, and boundaries of cleanliness. The idea was to build and retain the health of the Jewish community. Therefore, interethnic marriages were discouraged and had at times been strictly forbidden. Food boundaries were accomplished through kosher cooking. And many other rules were set up to keep unclean people and practices out of the community until and unless they could be purified. All of this was meant to promote and preserve the people of God. Ever since the mission of Jesus, the community of God has become bigger and, as Paul points out in Romans 1:12, is crucially important for our mutual encouragement in the faith.

Despite its importance, remaining in the community has not been easy. Much of Jesus's ministry was to heal the sick and forgive sinners so that they could rejoin their communities. Jesus preached that we should live life authentically by loving one another, and ever broaden our circles to include our neighbors. The irony of uncleanliness for the wealthy is that it is a self-identified condition that they then act on. Communities don't separate themselves from the wealthy, the wealthy separate themselves from the community. It is a self-inflicted symptom of *plutogenics*.

Becoming wealthy can cause us to become אָמֵט (unclean) in our hearts. This infection causes us to think we need separation from community. The *hoi polloi*, the *plebeians*, and the great unwashed become the terms used to describe the community from which the wealthy choose to separate. The masses are uneducated, are unhealthy, or simply don't have enough money to be properly arrogant. The gated community, private country clubs and private schools are all solutions to the "problem." This self-exile is motivated by fear— fear of robbery, fear of disease, and fear their children are not socializing with "their own kind." Their possessions make them susceptible to robbery and ransom. Their exposure to more people exposes them to contamination and disease. The interaction of their children with the common public does not enhance the opportunity for them to meet people of their parents' criteria.

This self-exile from everyday community denies contact with the diversity and social richness of everyday people. They miss the friendships made at public school activities. They miss the casual banter at the grocery store. They miss the freedom of running errands.

Proverbs 18:1 says, "Whoever isolates himself seeks his own desire; he breaks out against all sound judgment." Ultimately, it denies them the ability to join with others to become the body of Christ. Many celebrities confess that what they miss most as a result of their stardom is the ability to live a normal life in the community. The church is the community they can join to begin their healing.

Praise God for calling together the ἐκκλησία (*ekklésia*: an assembly, a [religious] congregation), where all distinctions are removed and "where Christ is all and in all" (Colossians 3:11). Where the ἐκκλησία meets is designated as a sanctuary from the outside world and all its fears. Collective worship can be the initial source of healing, while coming together in small groups with other brothers and sisters in Christ can provide the wealthy with joy and purpose. The small group is a balm where they can expose their true selves and rest—what a blessing!

THE TREATMENT AND CARE OF *PLUTOGENICS*

Salvation from *plutogenics* is found in the love of Jesus Christ and the grace of God. As Jesus observed when asked by his disciples how seemingly impossible it was to save a rich person, he stated in Mark 10:27, "With men it is impossible, but not with God; for with God all things are possible."

Pastors play an important role in reconciling people to Christ, and it is no different if they happen to be people who manage **surplus**. The challenge is that some pastors are confused about the economics of wealth from a theological point of view. They confuse the gifts of generating **surplus** with the disease of *plutogenics*. Because so many wealthy people exhibit the symptoms of the disease, they simply call for their extinction through renunciation and dissolution. They would have no more generators and distributors of **surplus**, without even a discussion or understanding of the consequences. Their conviction is a misunderstanding of the teachings of Jesus. As one Christian theologian states,

> Jesus' call for the elimination of wealth coupled with his emphasis on consuming only what one needs … is fundamentally incompatible with capitalism as currently practiced. Not only is the present system dependent upon relatively high, consistent levels of consumption in order to sustain itself, but it prioritizes rapid wealth generation and accumulation *above all else*.[84]

Until pastors can dispassionately learn exegetical economics, they will be as useful as a physician who is afraid of the sight of blood. Only then will they understand the difference and necessity of **surplus** versus the frailties of those in charge of it who are broadly labeled wealthy.

Physicians must take precautions when treating diseases and so should pastors—who are no more immune from *plutogenics* than doctors are from disease. Numerous investigations of TV evangelists have underscored this threat. The physician heals the sick of body and the pastor heals the sick of soul. The healing of *plutogenics* makes possible the healthy distribution of **surplus** that is so crucial to the church—and the pastor.

An understanding of exegetical economics will explain that budgets and

---

[84] Metzger, 195.

sabbaticals are paid from **surplus** not offering envelopes, just as milk comes from cows and not cartons. Some theologians conclude that "readers [of the Gospels] have had a very difficult time constructing a consistent viewpoint or set of instructions [regarding wealth]."[85] Such an admission explains the amplified confusion of their audience when they extrapolate their viewpoints in the area of economics, all the while invoking the authority of Jesus. Such pastors will be conflicted in their appeal for stewardship contributions, hating to deal with mammon. They should be insecure in providing economic counseling to dislocated members of their congregation, encouraging them to seek high payment for their gifts. They must deal with the conflict between their teachings and the economic actions of their everyday life.

How do they remain at peace as they accumulate evil wealth to pay for their cars, houses, education of their children, and their retirement? If they reject the economic system that sustains them, what does their conscience require? Do they relocate to a different system? How many pastors follow the radical teachings on wealth and capitalism they provide to others? Do they try to comfort their souls by pointing to others with more wealth?

Jesus expressed that the major failing of the religious leaders of his day was their hypocrisy. Wealth can be a scandal even for those who do not manage it.

Jesus addressed the problem at the beginning of his ministry. In Luke 4:23, he said, "You will surely say this proverb to Me, 'Physician, heal yourself!'" Applying this to himself surely binds it to his followers. Be sure you are not suffering from the disease that you are trying to diagnose and treat. Healing is an act of love, contained in the commandment of the Messiah himself when he said in Matthew 22:39, "You shall love your neighbor as yourself." But that command was predicated on the health of your love for God in verse 37. The command is an equation to love your neighbor equally as yourself. If your relationship with God is flawed then, despite your best intentions, the help you offer your neighbor will be flawed. The church is recognizing the need to reassess its understanding of faith and wealth and has called together assemblies to update their doctrines.

The first step in treating *plutogenics* more broadly is to immunize the pastor specifically. It is essential that pastors come to a foundational belief on exegetical economics as explained in scripture. They must form a broad paradigm of God's guidance relative to the creation and the human function $f(h)$. They must be able to discern the differences between **surplus** and the

---

[85] Ibid., 1.

wealthy. They must be able to articulate a personal relationship to the creation and to others that informs their own personal economic actions. Their lives must reflect integrity with their beliefs. At such a starting point and open to the continuing education of life itself, they are then able to engage the needs of their congregations.

Many times, a pastor will sense the disease of *plutogenics* in a wealthy member of the church who has not been responding to the financial needs of the church. This can be operating needs, mission needs, or capital campaigns. If the pastor himself has not been transformed as to **surplus** and its meaning, he may try the old approach of closing the sale through a special and personal plea. I think this misses the mark and may only result in giving without loving.

The pastor should see the need for the love of Jesus to grow in the member's heart. They need to join a small group and study the Bible. They need to meet with people serving in mission. Only when they understand the great love of God, and are filled with that love, are they prepared to respond to the vision of the pastor to grow and sustain the church. Then the giving will come from within and be a blessing to the giver, the pastor, and the church.

9

HEALTHY, WEALTHY, AND WISE

Praise the Lord.
Blessed are those who fear the Lord,
who find great delight in his commands.
Wealth and riches are in their houses
and their righteousness endures forever.

—Psalm 112:1, 3 (NIV)

This chapter will explore the blessings and responsibilities of those who have received the inoculation of grace regarding **surplus**.

Plato, channeling Socrates, explained his allegory of the cave by describing prisoners chained to only face a front wall, with a fire and partial wall behind them. On that partial wall, models of things were manipulated to project shadows on the wall in front of the chained prisoners. These shadows became their view and reality of the world. Through several stages of escape, one of the prisoners exits the cave to view creation in the natural light of the sun. He sees the truth of things rather than just their shadows. The experience is overwhelming, and he feels pity on his former fellow prisoners. He returns to describe his experience and the opportunity of escape from their dreary existence. The returning prisoner is in for a rough and frustrating ride.

This describes the challenge of a Christian who has experienced a walk with God and then tries to explain the joy and peace that is available to all. It is particularly challenging with a wealthy prisoner who has golden chains. As

Revelation 3:17 states, "They will say, 'I am rich, have become wealthy, and have need of nothing'—and do not know that [they] are wretched, miserable, poor, blind, and naked." Wealth does not prevent ignorance. Remember that these people are probably suffering from the blinding symptoms of *plutogenics*.

Each case of the disease will be different. It is well to follow the Hippocratic oath and "do no harm." Judgment and condemnation do not work here any better than on other sins. If you have had very little economic training, it may be best to identify a wealthy Christian member of the congregation to walk alongside them. They will be able to speak from experience to many of the questions of the suffering wealthy soul. They will be a visible model of a Christian disciple who built **surplus** in accordance with God's plan. Once accumulated, they distributed it in accordance with God's plan, thereby bearing fruit. The main idea is that we are all—including the wealthy—called to bear fruit, and we can only achieve that by attaching ourselves to Jesus and His plan.

My interpretation of John 15:5 is that we are all conduits. We don't originate love. We just pass it on. We fill ourselves with the love of Jesus and then distribute it to others. The wealthy, as managers of **surplus**, demonstrate this by being a conduit of **surplus** to demonstrate God's love.

This is the description of spiritually healthy, wealthy people: They realize that God's bounty does not originate with them, and they cannot truly possess it. It only passes through their lives. To grasp after it is to lose it. To hoard it is to clog the pipe until it bursts. To pour it out for the parched and dry, so that they may connect and grow and bear fruit, is their highest purpose and greatest joy. The sooner those that are productive enter into such an enterprise, the more fulfilling will be there life. Distributed **surplus** will not save souls *per se*, but it can demonstrate love.

Some see salvation as apart from our experience here on earth. We have to be separated from our bodies to begin an eternal union with God. We served and studied on Earth, but only death will provide Truth. That is how Benjamin Franklin understood it. In a 1790 letter, he said,

> I believe in one God, Creator of the Universe. That He governs it by His Providence. That he ought to be worshipped. That the most acceptable Service we render to him, is doing Good to his other Children. That the Soul of Man is immortal, and will be treated with Justice in another Life respecting its Conduct in this. ... As for Jesus of Nazareth ... I think

the system of Morals and Religion as he left them to us, the best the World ever saw … but I have … some Doubts to his Divinity; though' it is a Question I do not dogmatism upon, having never studied it, and think it is needless to busy myself with it now, where I expect soon an Opportunity of knowing the Truth with less Trouble.[86]

Alternatively, some contemporary theologians see continuity between this life and eternal. The insight is that the one may begin their participation right now in the eternal kingdom which was initiated by the resurrection of Jesus. This is the same kingdom that he will revisit and complete as a new creation. One such theologian, N. T. Wright, focuses on this already but not yet Kingdom of God—the chance to encounter in the here and now a glimmer of the eternal experience.

> The main meaning of the resurrection of Jesus for him [Paul] is that God's new world has been brought into being through this event, the long-promised new world in which the covenant will be renewed, sins will be forgiven and death itself will be done away with. The resurrection is neither an isolated and out-of-character divine miracle nor simply the promise of eternal life beyond the grave. It is, rather, the decisive start of the worldwide rule of the Jewish Messiah, in which sins are already forgiven and the promise of the eventual new world of justice and incorruptible life are assured.[87]

An understanding of the kingdom of God is crucial to those suffering from *plutogenics*. It is addressed head-on in the most celebrated scripture in the Bible about the quandary of the rich. In Mark 10:17-22, Matthew 19:16–22, and Luke 18:18–23, a rich young ruler approaches Jesus confidently. He seeks public affirmation of his salvation. Why not? He knows that he is a paragon of Jewish society. He may even have been a member of the Sanhedrin as Nicodemus or Joseph of Arimathea were, enjoying power and prestige. Now

---

[86] John Fea, "Religion and Early Politics: Benjamin Franklin and His Religious Beliefs," *Pennsylvania Heritage Magazine* 37, no. 4 (2011).

[87] N. T. Wright, *Surprised by Hope* (New York: HarperCollins, 2008), 247–8.

he sees his chance to be affirmed in front of the large crowds following Jesus on his way to Jerusalem. He may even have approached Jesus with flattery by calling him "good Teacher" as Mark and Luke attest. But Jesus uses it as a teaching moment for everyone who can hear. He did it in a gentle way. Mark suggests in a loving way. First Jesus points out that only God can be the absolute Good. Second, He allows the young man to proudly testify that he follows the Law, without exception, as a good Jew. Third, Jesus explains that to be perfect is to follow Him in total obedience. The young man would not. We all have things that we cling to in order not to obey Jesus. Jesus knew this young man suffered from *plutogenics* and his idol was his wealth. The young man silently hung his head.

This ended the discourse. The young man did not see Jesus as the Son of God, the Jewish Messiah, or even the chief priest of Israel. In his mind, he was inquiring of a charismatic rabbi. He chose not to obey. What was to be his great singular moment of public recognition turned into a difficult silence as he pivoted and walked away. He was sad. Once again, Jesus had made the outrageous, radical point that human intentions, motivations, works and celebrity are not sufficient to achieve salvation – not even for a perfect Jew. He had made the same point using the peerless John the Baptist as His example in Mathew 11:11.

"What happened?" cried his disciples as the young man departed. "He was rich and a pillar of society. Surely, observant, successful Jews will be saved." Jesus wanted to be absolutely clear. He used an old Jewish idiom for unthinkable thoughts. It had to do with passing through the eye of a needle. He expressed it with a camel, others expressed it with an elephant as noted in *Berakhot* 55b of the Talmud. Jesus was teaching that wealth is not an advantage in achieving salvation. The vast majority of people who manage **surplus** contract *plutogenics*. They take personal credit for their productivity, moderate consumption, and growing **surplus**. They hold themselves out for the admiration of society rather than giving God the glory. They do not realize that it is all vanity and they are but a vapor.

But then to the incredulous looks of his disciples and to our great joy, the Great Physician reiterated the gospel of grace. As recorded in Mark 10:27, Jesus said, "With men *it is* impossible, but not with God; for with God all things are possible" (NKJV). And He led them on to Jerusalem to make that gospel happen.

To this point, theologians generally agree on the understanding of the pericope. What they massively disagree on is what Jesus's remedy is for *plutogenics*. The disagreements stem in part from the fact that the three synoptic writers report the prescription slightly differently. Additionally, this is not the only time Jesus addresses this malady. But each time, he prescribes the same remedy. To get as clear an understanding as possible of what Jesus is suggesting, we must look at the various reports in this pericope as well as the remedies he suggested in the same circumstance on other occasions.

All three of the synoptic writers agree that the remedy focuses on distribution according to God's plan. The wealthy young man should create liquidity in order to give to the poor. In this way, he will be transferring his wealth from a limited, insecure, temporal setting into an eternal compounding heavenly IRA and, in so doing, allows himself to spend his earthly life in the company of Jesus. One of the three writers, Luke, says πάντα (*panta*: all)—sell all of your possessions. The others did not use that word. Many theologians use Luke's πάντα to argue the requirement for the renunciation of all wealth (**surplus**) for those who wish to be true disciples of Christ.

Others point to the *plutogenic* case of Zacchaeus in which the remedy of paying half of his possessions to the poor caused Jesus to say beginning in Luke 9:22, "Today salvation has come to this house, because he also is a son of Abraham; for the Son of Man has come to seek and to save that which was lost."

This group also points out that Peter never fully abandoned his ability to create **surplus** through fishing and returned to it, creating more **surplus** than ever before with Jesus's blessing in John 21. Similarly, Paul says in 1 Thessalonians that it is his ability to labor "night and day, that we might not be a burden to any of you" that afforded his ability to preach the gospel. So how are we to understand Jesus's remedy for *plutogenics*—total renunciation or Godly distribution?

The existential history of the church says both. Ignatius of Loyola, Francis of Assisi, and Teresa of Calcutta are all wonderful examples of total renunciation, the spreading of the gospel, and the growth of the church. But, like the original church of Jerusalem under James, their ministries would not have grown over the long term without the distribution of **surplus** from other Christians. From time to time in the history of the church a wealthy person is called to sell all of his possessions, give to the poor, and place himself at the mercy of others.

But if everyone who believed in Jesus stopped working, went to a street corner, and asked for support, would that help the widows and orphans that Jesus was so concerned about? Ephesians 4:28 makes a suggestion to thieves that is applicable to all: They "must work, doing something useful with their own hands, that they may have something to share with those in need."

Jesus never renounced the human function $f(h)$. He never said do not multiply. He supported an abundant life. His plan for humanity requires a constant state of **surplus**. That is why he told his disciples in the pericope of the young rich man, when they asked if the wealthy could be saved, that all things are possible with God. He will bless and evaluate on a case-by-case basis.

God's plan requires **surplus**, but its distribution will vary. Some he will call to renounce their wealth and do a one-time distribution. Most he will call to distribute their wealth continuously, as they continue to produce additional **surplus**. Scripture, pastors, and other Christians will be the vehicles God uses to reach each of them.

The good news for those suffering from *plutogenics* is that, as Jesus reported in the case of Zacchaeus, salvation is available today. Great amounts of **surplus** that are causing sores on the souls of too many will be released here and now to their great blessing. They will be shocked when a pastor who is offered a check says he will only accept it "if you come and follow me."

Taking them to the beneficiaries of their check, seeing the impact on their lives, and receiving their love and prayers will heal many. The "healthy wealthy" will become more focused on how to make their distribution more effective. The gifts they were given to generate the **surplus** will now come into play in its effective distribution. Most importantly, they will experience salvation—the eye of the needle will be in their rearview mirror. Along with N. T. Wright, they will participate in the kingdom here and now and have every joy in anticipating its completion. C. S. Lewis explains it this way:

> The good man's past begins to change so that his forgiven sins and remembered sorrows take on the quality of Heaven: the bad man's past already conforms to his badness and is filled only with dreariness. And that is why, at the end of all things, when the sun rises here and the twilight turns to blackness down there, the Blessed will say "We have never lived anywhere except in Heaven," and the Lost, "We were always in Hell." And both will speak truly.[88]

---

[88] C. S. Lewis, *The Great Divorce, a Dream* (London: G. Bles, 1945).

There are great Christians who were and are highly productive. God uses those with healthy souls to miraculous effect. And their lives will open to an abundance and joy that was not possible when they were merely wealthy. They see wealth as a means and not an end. Their end is to be "a Kingdom Builder rather than just a Wealth Builder." [89]

JESUS'S ECONOMIC TEACHINGS WERE CONSISTENT IN DISPARATE SITUATIONS

Jesus was not always successful in communicating the Gospel and what it meant on a day-to-day basis. But he kept at it offering observations and stories that passed on his thoughts from different angles. His teachings and contact with people did not enjoy the curation and universal publication of today's Bible. So, his activities, teachings, and observations were cumulative for only a few—those he spent day after day with—the twelve disciples. And when, halfway through his ministry, Jesus sat the twelve down in Caesarea Philippi to assess who the people understood him to be, only Peter confessed that he was "the Christ, the son of the living God." Jesus roared, "Blessed are you, Simon son of Jonah, for this was not revealed to you by flesh and blood, but by my Father in heaven. (Matt 16:16) So when Zacchaeus also got it, after a number of attempts by Jesus to explain Godly economics to others, Jesus roared, "Today salvation has come to this house, because this man, too, is a son of Abraham." (Luke 19:9)

What was it about Zacchaeus that was different from the temple givers of Mark 12:41–44 and Luke 21:1–4, the scribes and Pharisees of Mark 7:11, and the rich young businessman of Matt 19:16–22, Mark 10:17–22, Luke 18:18–23?

The Bible encourages giving to the poor, providing for familial support and inheritance as well as giving to the Temple. So, it is not the acts themselves that are a problem. And yet Jesus points out the hypocrisy of those performing those acts. The scriptures presuppose the acts are merely to obey the Torah, reflecting being a son of Abraham. But John the Baptist, as well as Jesus, stated that simply being a son of Abraham and performing works of the law are not sufficient for salvation.

As stated above, even the rich young businessman who came seeking eternal life through good works knew something more was required. He

---

[89] Warren, loc. 3469, Kindle.

wrongly associated goodness with salvation. Salvation is only available through the one good and perfect God. In the rich young man's mind, there must be some extraordinary work that would assure his salvation. He wanted Jesus to delineate such a work, a work that would be beyond those specified in the Torah, a work consistent with his identity as a rich young businessman.

In excruciating simplicity, Jesus explained the requirements of perfection. The perfection reflected only in God and Jesus. His successful persona would have to die. He would need to be "born again" as a humble follower and disciple of Jesus. By himself, he could not meet the test of perfection. Therefore, "he went away sorrowful for he had great possessions" (Matt. 19:22). In accordance with our model of the human function $f(h)$, we would say that the rich young businessman was neither willing to surrender his productivity nor his **surplus** to God.

Jesus points out in Mark 7:11, as well, that the scribes and Pharisees were not justly allocating their **surplus**. Instead of honoring their father and mother as required, they declared their **surplus** "corban" and reserved for the temple, only serving their own purposes. The human function $f(h)$ can also help us explain Jesus's observation in Mark 12. In speaking of the widow's offering, He said, "Truly I tell you, this poor widow has put more into the treasury than all the others." The others gave out of their **surplus**. But the poor widow sacrificed out of her consumption changing her standard of living.

How does the human function $f(h)$ help explain Jesus's roar of approval about Zacchaeus? It was Zacchaeus's statement, "Look, Lord! Here and now I give half of my possessions to the poor, and if I have cheated anybody out of anything, I will pay back four times the amount." Zacchaeus was not depending on his status as a son of Abraham nor solely distributing according to the Torah. He was submitting his productivity to the justness of God and being more generous with his **surplus** than required by the Law. He was doing this from his trust in Jesus. He became born again.

All of these teachings taken together, point to the requirement of faith in being born again and to surrender our production, our consumption, and finally our **surplus** to God. God wants all of us, all of the time. He wants us at work where we are productive. He wants us at home where we consume. He wants us as we distribute **surplus**. Only then can we be at peace that we are in God's will for us and experience the abundant life He promised.

A FINAL ADMONITION NOT TO BE "THAT GUY"

"That guy" is the pejorative designation for the person being used as a negative example. When the coach warns his players at the beginning of the season not to be "that guy," he is warning against behavior that disqualifies them from being on the team. Being "that guy" has consequences. You are no longer referred to by your personal name. You become a non-entity, an example. You are no longer part of the community. The Bible is full of admonitions not to be "that guy," but none quite so penetrating as a parable taught by Jesus, in which a rich man dies and pleads for a "do-over." It speaks to me personally. It grabs me as a warning from Jesus not to be "that guy." I will paraphrase it.

In Luke 16:19–31, we are told of a rich man who can afford to live in a gated community, buy any clothes he wants, and eats gourmet food. A poor, hungry man named Lazarus lies outside his gate. Ignored by the rich man, Lazarus receives compassion only from dogs who lick his sores. Both men die and find themselves in severely different circumstances. Lazarus is in community, protected, and loved by one of the Bible's richest patriarchs. The rich man is now in solitary confinement in a furnace. When he continues to act entitled by calling on Lazarus to serve him water, he is reminded of his obvious condition. There is an impassable chasm between him and Lazarus. It cannot be breached by either party despite their motivations. Finally contrite, the rich man begs for someone to go back to the living to save his brothers from becoming "that guy." But Jesus replies that some people, who haven't believed the warnings in the Bible, won't believe someone who has even risen from the dead. They, too, are condemned to be "that guy."

We don't have to be "that guy." The one who loses his personal identity and eternal relationship with God. We have the Bible to study. We have each other to be accountable to. We have the Holy Spirit speaking to us and through us. Sadly, those that become "that guy" for eternity are determined to abandon discipleship for the desire to claim "I did it my way." "My" is the most solitary and selfish expression in the English language. Don't be "that guy."

10
SURPLUS/WEALTH—
THEN AND NOW

Look! The wages you failed to pay the workers
who mowed your fields are crying out against you.
The cries of the harvesters have reached the ears of the Lord Almighty.
You have lived on earth in luxury and self-indulgence.
You have fattened yourselves in the day of slaughter.

—James 5:4–5 (NIV)

The processes to generate **surplus** have changed dramatically over the years as machines and then computers have leveraged human labor. Since production has moved on from one person driving others in manual labor, so has the connotation of exploitation in generating **surplus**. We will dive deeper into that issue in this chapter.

Many of the economic concepts—particularly productivity and wealth— that have been used in this book were understood differently in the time of Jesus. To better understand those concepts as he used them to teach eternal truths, we must have more context on the period of his ministry. There were several known ways to accumulate **surplus** and become wealthy in biblical times. You could grow it. You could trade for it. You could steal it. You could accumulate it through tithes, tribute, and taxes. You could take it through conquest. Jesus weighed in on all of these methods. He acknowledged the obligations of tithes, taxes, and tribute, but only in paying them. He specifically distanced himself from being a bandit, a thief, or a military messiah looking to seize worldly power. Jesus actively argued against all of the methods of acquiring **surplus** except successful agriculture and trade. But that did not mean building **surplus** was easy. In fact, to do it ethically was very hard.

Jesus's ministry encompassed the last three years of his life, concluding in AD 28. Historically, this is within the period of Second Temple Jerusalem. Those were hard economic times for the Jews. Rome ruled the country and Rome extracted tribute from all of the countries within its empire. Israel itself was already in a downward economic spiral in which no new land became available for cultivation and existing land ownership was consolidated at a rapid pace. During that period, the landed peasant was subject to a combined 40 percent assessment of his produce made up of Roman tribute, Jewish taxes, and temple tithes and offerings. There was no room for farming shortfall and marginal producers lost their land over time to larger Jewish aggregators of the Herodian class.[90] Drought years were common, and the social fabric between rich and poor became strained. Because of these conditions, there arose a broad swath of people engaged in social banditry. These were dispossessed farmers and laborers who would organize in gangs to raid village grain stores and government wagons carrying food tribute, tithes, and taxes. Some became quite notorious in the style of Jesse James or Robin Hood. Already in motion during Jesus's ministry, this economic recession would only get worse in the following years in which James, his brother, led the Jerusalem church.

But even in these tough times there were people who built **surplus** ethically. Jesus did not condemn such people—including the rich young ruler, Joseph of Arimathea, or Zacchaeus once he repented. His parables often used rich landowners as similes for God. But ethical rich people were in the minority. Most rich people grew and sustained their **surplus** through economic oppression of the people. We will now turn to some modern economic models to better understand the ethics of the situation.

There is a part of economics that studies the decisions that rational people face (both conflicting and cooperating) when interacting with each other under a given set of assumptions. It is called game theory and is not to be confused with algorithms for video games. Economic game theory allows real-world practitioners of political science, psychology, and economics

---

[90] Richard A. Horsley and John S. Hanson, *Bandits, Prophets & Messiahs: Popular Movements in the Time of Jesus* (Harrisburg: Trinity Press International, 1999), 56.

to predict outcomes based on certain assumptions and prime actions. The particular model within game theory that we find useful in understanding the economics of Second Temple Jerusalem is called the zero-sum game. The primary assumption is that the total amount of desired goods is finite and fixed. The actions of the prime actor in taking goods from the finite supply impact the amount of goods that remain for all of the other actors. The ethics of a powerful prime actor is determined by how much of the goods he takes and his rationale. To take just enough of the goods to subsist would leave a maximum amount of remaining goods for the other actors and would be termed ethical. To take a very large amount of the goods to arbitrarily build his personal **surplus** while leaving a minimal amount of goods for the other actors would be termed unethical. As the prime actor "wins" by taking more of the goods, the other actors "lose" by receiving fewer of the goods since the total amount of goods is fixed.

The application of the zero-sum game is very straightforward in the agrarian economy in the time of Jesus and James. Because of drought conditions, the harvest might be marginal and fixed. Because of the land aggregation, there would be one owner but many workers. There would be many more unemployed workers, thus depriving those hired of having any bargaining power. The owner, as the first actor, would take an arbitrary amount of the harvest, which would build his personal **surplus** or wealth. The remaining food would be split many times down to a bare subsistence level and sometimes be delayed. Building wealth through economic oppression is always wrong. It was wrong in AD 62, the time of James, and it is wrong today. Listen to how James reacts to the practice:

> [1]Now listen, you rich people, weep and wail because of the misery that is coming on you. [2]Your wealth has rotted, and moths have eaten your clothes.[3] Your gold and silver are corroded. Their corrosion will testify against you and eat your flesh like fire. You have hoarded wealth in the last days. [4]Look! The wages you failed to pay the workers who mowed your fields are crying out against you. The cries of the harvesters have reached the ears of the Lord Almighty. [5]You have lived on earth in luxury and self-indulgence. You have fattened yourselves in the day of slaughter. [6]You have

condemned and murdered the innocent one, who was not opposing you.[91]

Jesus did not preach the zero-sum game being practiced in the first century AD. He preached charity through the distribution of **surplus**. John the Baptist emplified him in Luke 3:11 saying, "Anyone who has two shirts should share with the one who has none, and anyone who has food should do the same."

There was another kind of economic activity that was thought unethical. It was local retail trade—the exchange of goods within a given community as opposed to an exchange of goods between communities separated by time and distance. Remember, it was largely a barter economy. And, as demonstrated by the Hammurabi Stele, goods had an intrinsic set value. That meant that there should be no negotiation in bartering since all combinations of exchanged goods were fixed. The expectation that in such an exchange neither party would be economically better or worse off after the trade. There would be no **surplus** accrued to either party. So, if a person did create **surplus** in such a retail activity, they would be guilty of some unethical activity. This would be the Marshallian concept of **surplus**. It might be that the horse they traded was lame, a fact unknown to the other party. It might be that one party extorted a higher than intrinsic value in the exchange due to the desperation of the other party. As a result, there was a myriad set of rules compiled to insure a neutral exchange. For instance, one must not mix the poor vegetables with the superior vegetables from another field. One must not place the best fruit at the top of the barrel representing the same quality when poorer fruit lay below. There were many, many such ethical rules.[92] The ethical problems intrinsic to retail trade had been pointed out in the fourth century BC. Aristotle held disdain for retail trading, which he called χρηματιστική (*chrematisticae*: commerce), as a means to build **surplus** or wealth. The church would hold this view for centuries after Jesus.

Does the application of these economic models and issues of retail trade to our contemporary economy proclaim the same problems with building **surplus** and wealth? While limited cases of the zero-sum game can be found, generally the amounts of food, goods and services are not fixed. The gross national product (GDP) continues to grow. Productivity through

---

[91] Barker, ed.

[92] Neusner, 88.

technology is growing at an ever-increasing rate. Consider the farmer of today using mechanization and modern cultivation methods to create vastly more food than hundreds of farmers could grow in the time of Jesus. Enough food to feed his family, pay all of his workers fairly and on time, and still build a substantial **surplus**. The zero-sum game does not fit the larger world economy.

Likewise, retail trade has completely changed. We operate in a free market. Goods used in exchange do not have an intrinsic value but a utility value assigned by the participants. Each participant's utility of the same good may be different. The measure of an ethical retail transaction is that each participant's utility be greater after the transaction. Remember, in the time of Jesus, the criterion for a fair retail transaction was that each participant be no better or worse off intrinsically than before the trade. Many retail transactions are made long distance over the internet without first examining the product. Such transactions are possible because of the liberal return policies, protected pay methods and extended warranties on the products. Consequently, if Apple can build a phone with a very high utility for the consumer, and yet through technology build it at a low cost, they will accrue great **surplus** through ethical retail trade.

The growth of technology in capitalist economies is so great that vast amounts of **surplus** and wealth are being created. Wealth today requires a more nuanced understanding. **Surplus** creation due to productivity benefits everyone in the process. More analysis is required to understand the manner in which the **surplus** was generated, how it is managed, and how it is distributed. Theologians still stuck in the legacy understanding of wealth creation in the time of Jesus think it is still a pejorative. Those theologians who recognize that God has given some people a special gift of productivity to generate such **surplus** will focus on the teachings of Jesus to influence the distribution of that **surplus** for God's plan and glory.

11
THE CHURCH ON EXEGETICAL ECONOMICS

Keep watch over yourselves and all the flock
of which the Holy Spirit has made you overseers.
Be shepherds of the church of God,
which he bought with his own blood.

—Acts 20:28 (NIV)

Jesus laid the responsibility on Peter to "feed my sheep." That charge has been passed down through apostolic succession to leaders of the church today. In this chapter, we will examine how those teachings regarding wealth and money have change over the years and created fertile soil for an expanded dialogue using exegetical economics.

Theologians of the church all have the same goal—to help Christians understand how God would have them live for his glory and their salvation. God makes such things known through general revelation, the wonder of the creation, and special revelation—the scriptures. An initial task began with explaining the relationship of Jesus to God, the nature of Jesus himself, and the realm of the Holy Spirit.

It wasn't easy arriving at the Trinity and the concept that three is one. But it is a human model. The Trinity, which informs what we believe and how we live, is nowhere explicitly expressed in the Bible. Yet, we pray to a

Father, walk with Jesus, and listen internally to the Holy Spirit—all equally authoritative. But it took an emperor with all of the authority and threat he could muster to drive the process.

Similarly, we do not have an economic model explicitly expressed in the Bible. The commandments in the Bible to rest the land and animals are consonant with what we feel inside, perhaps from the Holy Spirit. The wondrous creation was made out of love for us and to sustain us. We should protect it and not cause it to become ill and fail.

Thus, our first exegetical economic equation was $C_v = \beta_0 + \beta_1 f(h)_i + G_i$. We should be concerned about living our lives in such a way that the creation can rejuvenate to support an increasing population. Many in the world have recognized for some time the impact of human activity on the environment. Some might even criticize the church for being late to the party—especially since scripture raised this concern over three thousand years ago. Fortunately, we now have nations coming together to discuss the issue such as in the Paris Agreement on Climate. But the issues are complex and require negotiation as to who must do what in the future. This time we do not have an emperor who is putting his weight behind a consensus.

To its credit, the church has engaged the subject driven by a social justice perspective. Mistreating the creation impacts the marginal in societies first who must live with the pollution waste and degraded landscape on a disproportionate basis. Pope Francis poses the challenge in the form of an "integral ecology." The bond between humans and the natural world means that we live in an "integral ecology," and as such, an integrated approach to environmental and social justice is required.[93]

I interpret him to say, in terms of the exegetical economic model, that in addition to recognizing the first theorem of creation vitality, we must accomplish the task through a just modification of the human function $f(h)$. The obvious way in economic terms would be to include the cost of environmental recycling and rejuvenation in the total cost of production. This is termed "all-in" pricing, which would not allow the low-cost producer to shift some of his costs to society at large by dumping waste and ravaging the environment for free. It is a big idea and would have to be implemented and monitored by governments around the world. Rational consumers compare prices, so all goods would have to have the "all-in" label.

The Vatican has taken the lead on these issues forming two Pontifical

---

[93] Ramanathan, 747.

Academies. One, focusing on the natural sciences, will deal with our first theorem $C_v = \beta_0 + \beta_1 f(h)_i + G_i$. The second academy comprised of social scientists presumably will be dealing with our second theorem $f(h)$ the human function of **Production - Consumption = Surplus**. They are both intellectually consonant with the definition of exegetical economics by looking to bring change within the confines of its relationships. In 2014, following a meeting of both academies, they concluded, "The resolution of major environmental problems facing society requires a fundamental reorientation in our behavior and attitude toward nature and toward each other."[94] I believe having a model such as provided in this book would be helpful in keeping such a discussion coherent and on track. We will look further into human systems of organization in the chapter entitled "Normative Economics."

In the final instance, exegetical economics is microeconomics. It is based on the smallest unit of economic decision making—the individual. While macroeconomics does deal with group activity such as government policy concerning taxes, budgets, and interest rates, and corporate policy concerning production, wages, and dividends, they are both driven through a decision-making process involving individuals. Those individuals are informed by their worldviews and foundational beliefs. It is possible for companies to reflect the Christian tenets of its owner. But in larger corporations and certainly countries, the constituency is a reflection of society—Christians, other faiths, and nonbelievers. This should not dismay Christians for they should continue to walk in faith and joy even as they work in cooperation with others. Augustine of Hippo saw this when he talked about the earthly city and the heavenly city.

> Thus, the things necessary for this mortal life are used by both kinds of men and families alike, but each has its own peculiar and widely different aim in using them. The earthly city, which does not live by faith, seeks an earthly peace, and the end it proposes, in the well-ordered concord of civic obedience and rule, is the combination of men's wills to attain the things which are helpful to this life. The heavenly city, or rather the part of it which sojourns on earth and lives

---

[94] Ibid.

by faith, makes use of this peace only because it must, until this mortal condition which necessitates it shall pass away.[95]

The church, rightly so, has concentrated on the individual—their relationship with God and their eternal salvation. While the church is guided by scripture in this endeavor there is disagreement in what it has to say.

As a consequence, the history of the church on its teachings regarding **surplus** has boiled down to an agreement to disagree. Some feel that a total and complete separation from **surplus** is required to be a true disciple of Christ. This is called radical renunciation and involves solemn and eternal vows to God. Others feel that people must stay practically employed to produce, modestly consume, and generate **surplus**. That **surplus** should not be disavowed but rather distributed in accordance with divine teaching. This is called almsgiving. Alms are portions of one's **surplus** given to the church to further God's Kingdom, including the poor and marginalized.

Radical renunciation versus almsgiving is a continuing debate. It caused a great schism in the religious, serving the church, regarding the perfect life model—the monastic life as opposed to the parish life. The issue of wealth and power was fundamental to the Avignon papacy and simultaneous popes. Transfer of **surplus** to the church via indulgences was an igniter for the Reformation. The accretion of monastic wealth was certainly a motivator for Henry VIII's Monastic Dissolution. The details of this and much more in the history of the church are wonderfully described by others. I have found Justo Gonzalez's book, *Faith and Wealth*, both comprehensive and balanced. Rather than repeat what others have presented, I would like to focus on how those issues are expressed and debated today.

Radical renunciation still has a stentorian, but minor voice in the church. I have found James A. Metzger's voice in his book, *Consumption and Wealth in Luke's Travel Narrative*, sincere and scholarly from a theological point of view. But his laudatory thanks to those wealthy entities that provided the **surplus** (my word) that sustained him in his sabbatical to write the book seemed inconsistent with his argument. Did a lack of economic training prevent him from seeing the cognitive dissonance of his existential situation and the thesis of his book? But I do recommend his book to others who are interested in taking a vow of poverty and entering a religious order.

---

[95] Augustine, Henry Scowcroft Bettenson, and G. R. Evans, *Concerning the City of God against the Pagans*, new ed. (London: Penguin, 2003), loc. 13089–93, Kindle.

That option remains today for those that feel refuge from the secular world is required to bring them closer to God. The monastic life has been diminishing in participation since its zenith in the late middle ages. Some of the reasons for its decline are theological, brought about by the Reformation, and some are economic in that they did not create enough **surplus** for growth relative to parish communities. Providing for the expression of both radical renunciation and almsgiving, the church has largely turned its focus on the issue of building **surplus** per se.

Henri Nouwen, ordained a Catholic priest, continues to be a guiding light to priests and pastors alike even as he has passed. His theology, honed from teaching at the University of Notre Dame, Yale Divinity School, and Harvard Divinity School, has been published in more than forty books translated into twenty-two languages. His psychological training provided unique tools to explore and beautifully communicate the depths of human emotion in parables such as The Prodigal Son.[96] But it was his lifestyle, having taken religious vows which included poverty, and living his final years as companion and pastor to a L'Arche community of mentally handicapped people that manifested Christ in his life to all. Nouwen saw a rift in the church caused by money and wealth, between those that have it and those that don't. He saw lurking in the heart of some religious a "prejudice against the rich."

> Perhaps we think the rich have more money than they deserve, or that they got their wealth at the expense of the poor. Maybe we find it hard to love the rich as much as the poor. But nobody says we should love the rich less than we love the poor. The poor are indeed held in the heart of God. We need to remember that the rich are held there too. I have met a number of wealthy people over the years. More and more, my experience is that rich people are also poor, but in other ways.[97]

Nouwen felt that a "conversion" is required for all those who need to deal with wealth in a healthy fashion. Such a conversion "means to experience a

---

[96] Henri J. M. Nouwen, *The Return of the Prodigal Son* (New York: Doubleday, 1994).

[97] Henri J. M. Nouwen, "The Spirituality of Fund-Raising," in *Henri Nouwen Society*, ed. Estate of Henri J. M. Nouwen (Richmond Hill: Upper Room Ministries, 2004), 18.

deep shift in how we see and think and act"[98] about wealth. A conversion for both those who feel wealth has no place in the church and those who have made it their idol and sole security. Such a conversion would bring many together, shoulder to shoulder, for the mission of the church. However, a more comprehensive solution would be to provide education to both groups such that they could work together at an earlier stage avoiding erroneous prejudicial tendencies in the first place. It is our feeling that an understanding of exegetical economics will provide the necessary tools to understand how to manage and distribute **surplus** and to perceive those with the "Joseph gift" in a spiritually healthy way.

Building a better understanding of scriptural support for issues regarding wealth and justice draws large and diverse Christian groups together to find common agreement. Reminiscent of the Westminster Divines of 1643 made up of theologians and parliamentarians, "over one hundred theologians and economists, ethicists and development practitioners, church leaders and business managers" came together in 1990 in Oxford, England, to discuss faith, economics, and justice. The product of their work is known as the "Oxford Declaration on Christian Faith and Economics." What brought this diverse group together can be seen in their universal affirmation of major theological points:

- God pronounced the whole creation good.
- God is the ultimate owner.
- The thoughtlessness, greed, and violence of sinful human beings have damaged God's good creation and produced a variety of ecological problems and conflicts.
- Economic production results from the stewardship of the earth which God assigned to humanity. While materialism, injustice, and greed are in fundamental conflict with the teaching of the whole Scripture, there is nothing in Christian faith that suggests that the production of new goods and services is undesirable.

They used these affirmations to reach conclusions in today's technological age. Fundamentally they asserted that technology is both good and also presents the opportunity for extensive evil.

They caution, "We must not allow technological development to follow

---

[98] Ibid., 4.

its own inner logic, but must direct it to serve moral ends." Their approach to work becomes a bit fuzzy as they stretch the meaning to simultaneously cover aspects of economic thought on earth and theological thought in terms of fostering God's work. They conclude, "Sin makes work an ambiguous reality. It is both a noble expression of human creation in the image of God, and, because of the curse, a painful testimony to human estrangement from God."

The document rightly summarizes that "Christians everywhere [are called] to place high priority on restoring and maintaining the integrity of creation." They also point out that poverty results from "the evil that people do to each other, to themselves, and to their environment." They call on "those who are gifted by the Spirit and whose actions are guided by the demands of love" to become involved in socio-political activities in order to address poverty directly.[99]

A different conclave sponsored by the Lausanne Movement and Business as Mission Global came together in Chiang Mai, Thailand, in March 2017. About thirty people from business, the church, missions, and academia created a declaration entitled "The Role of Wealth Creation for Holistic Transformation." It made thirteen very straightforward affirmations:

- Wealth creation is rooted in God the Creator, who created a world that flourishes with abundance and diversity.
- We are created in God's image, to co-create with him and for him, to create products and services for the common good.
- Wealth creation is a holy calling, and a God-given gift, which is commended in the Bible.
- Wealth creators should be affirmed by the church, and equipped and deployed to serve in the marketplace among all peoples and nations.
- Wealth hoarding is wrong, and wealth sharing should be encouraged, but there is no wealth to be shared unless it has been created.
- There is a universal call to generosity, and contentment is a virtue, but material simplicity is a personal choice, and involuntary poverty should be alleviated.
- The purpose of wealth creation through business goes beyond giving generously, although that is to be commended; good business has

---

[99] Cathrin M. van Sintern, "The Oxford Declaration on Christian Faith and Economics (1990): Vorgeschichte, Analyse, Rezeption Und Ausblick" (master's thesis, Oxford Centre for Mission Studies and University of Wales, 2003).

intrinsic value as a means of material provision and can be an agent of positive transformation in society.

- Business has a special capacity to create financial wealth, but also has the potential to create different kinds of wealth for many stakeholders, including social, intellectual, physical and spiritual wealth.
- Wealth creation through business has proven power to lift people and nations out of poverty.
- Wealth creation must always be pursued with justice and a concern for the poor, and should be sensitive to each unique cultural context.
- Creation care is not optional. Stewardship of creation and business solutions to environmental challenges should be an integral part of wealth creation through business.

All of this they affirm in order encourage holistic transformation of people and societies to produce more wealth-creators and to encourage them "to perseverance, diligently using their God-given gifts to serve God and people."[100]

Neither of these assemblies contradicted each other. However, there is certainly a very different tone to each one. Clearly, the Lausanne Movement did not feel the Oxford group recognized and encouraged "wealth" creation sufficiently. Ron Sider, founder and president emeritus of Evangelicals for Social Action and a distinguished professor at Palmer Seminary at Eastern University, commenting on the Lausanne work finds, "While this manifesto is reflective of important biblical themes, it ignores others and ultimately fails to provide the balanced wisdom and guidance so urgently needed on this important topic.[101] It lacks the biblical warnings about wealth generation and the need for justice in its distribution.

The different tones of these two declarations remind me of the business theorem to have your own attorney write the first draft of the contract. It is in the control of the drafting that the tenor of the discussions is summarized. The discussions themselves may have been much more wide-ranging with several minority positions. Such discussions of businesspeople and theologians, brought together by a love for Jesus and for the glory of God, are the kind

---

[100] "Wealth Creation Manifesto," Lausanne Movement, https://www.lausanne.org/content/wealth-creation-manifesto.

[101] Ron Sider, "The Holy Calling of Wealth Creation Isn't So Simple," *Christianity Today*, August 24, 2017.

of settings where the exegetical economic model could be useful. It would minimize the use of words like "work," "wealth," and "sin" which have long-standing legacies of meaning in theology, and use more objective economically defined terms such as "productivity," "consumption," and "**surplus**." Even a newly coined word such as *plutogenics* can help us get out of a rut and show how to point out the very real dangers in managing **surplus**. It would then be possible to be more precise in our communication.

I believe such improvement in communications would identify ideas of agreement more quickly without the requirement to rephrase every proposition to our own understanding of legacy words. More time could be spent on how to address the issues of **surplus** encouragement and just distribution going forward.

12
NORMATIVE ECONOMICS

He said to them, "Therefore every teacher of the law
who has become a disciple in the kingdom of heaven
is like the owner of a house who brings out of his storeroom
new treasures as well as old."

—Matthew 13:52 (NIV)

Even before Plato, philosophers were opining on human society and the way it should be. This chapter will look at the issue of past thoughts on "the right economic system" and what the Bible tells us about various economic systems.

The economics that most of us studied in school and talk about today can be classified as positive economics. We think of it as something that can be measured and tested. We talk of models that explain how we interact and expect that they are predictive of future actions. Another branch of economics has been defined in modern times, although its contributors go back to antiquity. It is called normative economics and is based on personal criteria of how an economy should function. Because it is subjective and value-based it is not subject to testing and proof. It is theoretical. It is hypothetical. It can be debated endlessly.

While the term normative economics is new, the concept of "appropriate" economics is as old as Aristotle's comparison of οἰκονομία (*oikonomía*), which he viewed as ethical, honest farm labor to accumulate **surplus** versus χρηματιστική (*chrematistica*), which he viewed as unethical retail exchange and banking to accumulate **surplus**.

However, as the economy of the world evolved from command economies to marketplace economies, surpluses began to grow and be reemployed in production. As the wealthy reinvested the **surplus** into newly invented, productive machines, the age of industrialization was born. The industrial economy had many problems associated with it including exploiting manual labor, monopolies, and a blossoming of *plutogenics*.

These problems were identified by economists such as Karl Marx and Friedrich Engels. Their normative economic theories were actually put into play through revolution. By passing from normative to positive their results became measurable. We now evaluate various positive economic systems using the exegetical economic model of the human function $f(h)$ previously defined.

ASCETIC ENCLAVES

The solemn vow of "poverty, chastity, and obedience" uttered by Francis of Assisi in the twelfth century was a normative economic code that had been tried on several other ancient occasions. They have proved to be a governor on the human function $f(h)$ at large. Growth through accretion has been surpassed by organic growth ever since the time of the Essenes.

While such a community can provide a sanctuary for the individual, they grow only through the acquisition of new initiates. The broader church has always recognized the sanctity of life which is consonant with a growth in population. As we have seen, such growth is only possible in a state of sustained **surplus**.

Consequently, the church's primary focus since the Reformation has been attending to the spiritual needs of the growing population outside of monasteries. That has caused it to grapple with the economic reality of **surplus** (wealth). The church sees a world where punishing poverty continues despite a growing **surplus**. Some theologians term this disparity as a lack of economic justice. They see intentional systematic oppression as opposed to individual human frailty. Their zeal plunges them into economic theory and radical proposals with little or no economic training.

Since their own experiences have largely been capitalism, its weaknesses and faults have been readily apparent. They tend to promote the theoretical benefits of other systems while looking for exegetical support from scripture. I do not believe scripture supports any specific economic system as experienced by humankind since the Garden of Eden. In fact, God's plan for humankind has survived and perpetuated through all human systems.

I believe God will support and sustain any human economic system only insofar as it reflects his exegetical economic model. We will not arrive at a Kingdom economic system until Jesus returns to institute one. Let's examine some human economic systems in light of the exegetical economic model.

COMMUNISM

Communism is defined as a system in which goods are owned in common and are available to all as needed. It has been a normative theory that some say would create a utopian society. Some find scriptural support for communism.

The definition of communism matches up beautifully with words found within Acts 4. Verse 32 states, "Now the multitude of those who believed were of one heart and one soul; neither did anyone say that any of the things he possessed was his own, but they had all things in common."

Verse 35 concludes, "And laid them at the apostles' feet; and they distributed to each as anyone had need." And God used this system. Verse 33 states, "And with great power the apostles gave witness to the resurrection of the Lord Jesus. And great grace was upon them all."

Of course, none of this obviated Genesis 3:19, and it took work to eat in first-century Palestine. The Jerusalem Church was disconnected from both the Temple distributions by the Sanhedrin and the ability to farm by the Romans. They depended wholly on the liquidation of previously generated **surplus**. Consequently, the system described in Acts 4 and the Essene community before them are better termed as "lifeboat" economies. That is an isolated group surrounded by a hostile environment depending on the assets provided by the members in the boat.

In a lifeboat situation, the first thing you do is inventory everything everyone has and designate it as commonly owned. You then use whatever is in the inventory to maximize the survivability of the whole boat population. All the possessions given to the apostles in Acts 4 and 5 were produced in the broader command economy. The people brought it into the boat with them. Because of the hostile Romans, Jewish Sanhedrin, and even consecutive droughts, no one in the early church was in a position to generate **surplus** and provide sustained internal support.

They were fortunate enough to bring people into their boat from as far away as Cyprus to keep it afloat. Paul's efforts to raise donations for the Jerusalem church on his various mission trips certainly extended the life of the church. But the model could not perpetuate itself. Peter would go on to Antioch and ultimately Rome. He would be the leader in all the churches that he visited. And yet he did not try and duplicate the economic system described in Acts 4 and 5.

We turn now to the exegetical economic model, where $f(h)$ is **production - consumption = surplus**, for a better understanding of this. Examining the human function $f(h)$, we see that Production is the first requirement. In the lifeboat economy, there is no production. There is only the acquisition of **surplus** that individuals operating in contiguous, but different economies generated.

While it may not be a viable earthly model, it may be what is experienced in heaven. In heaven God provides, and he does so generously with great **surplus**. Papius, the famous eye-witness to the resurrection chronicler, reported about heaven:

> The days will come when vines will grow, each having ten thousand shoots, and on each shoot ten thousand branches, and on each branch ten thousand twigs, and on each twig ten thousand clusters, and in each cluster ten thousand grapes, and each grape when crushed will yield twenty-five measures of wine. And when one of the saints takes hold of a cluster, another cluster will cry out, I am better, take me, bless the Lord through me. Similarly a grain of wheat will produce ten thousand heads, and every head will have ten thousand grains, and every grain ten pounds of fine flour, white and clean. And the other fruits, seeds, and grass will produce in similar proportions, and all the animals feeding on these fruits produced by the soil will in turn become peaceful and harmonious toward one another, and fully subject to humankind. ... These things are believable to those who believe.[102]

With production removed as a concern, it was the total justice of

---

[102] Irenaeus, *Five Books of S. Irenaeus: Bishop of Lyons, against Heresies*, Library of Fathers of the Holy Catholic Church (Oxford: J. Parker, 1872), 5.33.3–4.

distribution of the **surplus** that the early church modeled. The Apostles took on the role of the wealthy and made the distribution decisions. Guided by the Holy Spirit, they distributed the amount that was appropriate for the consumption of each individual. But distribution of **surplus** in not an option without production. Again, we live in a world where God ordained in Genesis 3:19, "In the sweat of your face you shall eat bread Till you return to the ground, For out of it you were taken; For dust you are, And to dust you shall return." Absolute communism has never been viable on a large scale for an extended period of time here on earth; we will know more in heaven.

SOCIALISM

Socialism came about as an imperfect but necessary first step toward Communism. That is how Karl Marx and Friedrich Engels justified the Soviet Union resulting from the Bolshevik revolution of 1917. Socialism is an economy similar to communism, where the entire society as a whole, through its elite, owns the means of production, allocates consumption, and distributes the **surplus**.

This is accomplished through government ownership of all manufacturing organizations and equipment. It also controls the market of exchange for goods and services. The government makes the decisions of how to allocate **surplus** between economic growth, education, health, defense, and all other societal needs. The USSR arose through a militant minority, not an election by the majority. It arose through the critical examination of capitalism and its many shortcomings. Socialism has proven not to be a path to Communism. However, it has proven to be a sustainable economic model in totalitarian and democratic countries.

The pinnacle of Soviet socialism may have been in the 1956 when Premier Khrushchev boldly predicted, "We will bury you!" Taken by many in the West as a military threat, a full contextual translation interprets his statement as an economic boast: "We will be here after your funeral." Khrushchev, who fully concluded that socialism and capitalism were mutually exclusive, expected socialism to outlast and supersede capitalism. It did not turn out that way. From a scope and participation standpoint, socialism has been losing ground to capitalism on a continuing basis.

The Soviet Union and China are the two largest examples of change. However, there are a number of Western countries with very high standards of living who practice a form of socialism today.[103] From a theological standpoint socialism has been seen as atheistic or humanistic. Avowed socialists (nee communists) have associated religion as the "opium of the people" found in capitalist societies to insure domestication of the masses. Humanist, socialist countries simply feel that humans are fully capable and motivated to provide everything humanity needs.

Let us evaluate socialism in the context of exegetical economics, where the human function $f(h)$ is defined as **production - consumption = surplus**. Such a comparison is a challenge because there are different forms of socialism and they have changed over time. Socialist production was originally tightly controlled by a centralized bureaucracy. The Five-Year Plans of the Soviet Union and the Great Leap Forward of China were based on the knowledge and execution of very few "experts" at the top. Their inefficiencies in the allocation of resources hit productivity hard. Bureaucratic assessment of consumer preferences and needs was not well received by the broader populace, creating discontent and waste. The inefficiencies and waste combined to reduce the overall **surplus** and consequently distribution available for societal needs.

Their human function $f(h)$ was so inefficient that the people demanded changes. But perhaps the most flagrant failing of socialism is that the distribution can be very unjust. The "wealthy" elite who make the distribution decisions in Russia and China live a very different lifestyle than the populace they control. This elite suffers from *plutogenics* in major ways without the grace of God to heal.

As previously pointed out, there are a number of western democracies who practice different forms of socialism. To different degrees they place a light bureaucratic hand on production. They allow private property and a free marketplace in most sectors of the economy to drive the quantity and quality of goods produced and consumed. They generally reserve the sectors of education, health, and defense for total government direction. Building and controlling the **surplus** is their major goal. They do this by applying very high taxes to income which reduces consumption and private **surplus** and adds to the government **surplus**. The democratically elected socialist governments emphasize broader education and health services from the distributions of their **surplus** than do the more capitalist economies. This forced leveling of consumption and provision of broader education

---

[103] China, Denmark, Finland, Netherlands, Canada, Sweden, Norway, Ireland, e.g.

and health services makes for a stronger social fabric and less social tension. These countries teach and preach a secularist humanistic worldview, but they generally allow freedom of religion. In addition to the reduction of consumption, the high taxes also reduce individual charity and church support. For comparison purposes using our exegetical economic model, where the human function $f(h)$ is **production** − **consumption** = **surplus**, we would observe that production represented by GDP (gross domestic product) has not grown as fast as in socialist economies as it has in more capitalist economies. The government bureaucrats who have the great power to redistribute are frequently corrupted. There remains a wide disparity in lifestyles in these economies and a fertile environment for *plutogenics* to flourish.

CAPITALISM

Capitalism is an economic system whereby property and other factors of production are privately owned and voluntarily exchanged for mutual benefit through a marketplace. The system benefits from a division of labor in which people gravitate to what they do best. This highest and best use of their gifts generates their maximum production. When combined with moderate consumption, it generates the largest surpluses. As a person builds a **surplus** of a specific item, their marginal utility for that item decreases. Finding a trading partner with a similar situation regarding a different good, they make a mutual exchange trading a less desirable good for a more desirable good in each case. Thus, both parties come out better for the transaction. This system has generated huge amounts of **surplus** which allows for greater reinvestment in R&D to make even more goods. This virtuous cycle of achieving more **surplus**, which in turn builds productivity through reinvestment, has still allowed for the greatest increase in mass consumption in the history of the world. Sufficient basic food and clothing for the entire population have been achieved by capitalist societies for a period of time. The profit motive drives the capitalist system. It is the corporate expression of the human function $f(h)$. Profit is an expression of revenue minus costs. Profits earned by a company are organizational **surplus** and accrue to the owners of that company. The owners can be a single family or thousands of people who own stock in the company. Such a system favors entrepreneurs who can anticipate the needs of large groups of consumers and build products to satisfy high demand. This also means that capitalism creates the largest disparity in societal incomes and

surplus (wealth). When we look at our exegetical economic model where the human function $f(h)$ is **production - consumption = surplus**, we see that production seems to have no bounds under capitalism. More and more people enter the system educated and trained to do what they do best. Consumption rises for all but much more for a few. Still, the production outpaces the consumption and the **surplus** continues to grow. The growing **surplus** of capitalism is weighing on the souls of those in charge of its distribution and *plutogenics* has reached epidemic proportions. *Plutogenics* has exploited what some hoped would be a utopian *laissez-faire* (unregulated) marketplace. But the creation of monopolies, cornering markets, and other frauds required the government to intervene in order to provide a fair and orderly marketplace. Additionally, the uneven buildup of **surplus** has caused the government to institute progressive income taxes and subsidize healthcare and education for the populace to maintain the social fabric. Most see this as just and appropriate. What makes the United States standout as a capitalist country is the amount of **surplus** that is allowed to remain private property under the control of the individual. The battle for distribution rages on between progressives, who feel it should be by the government, and the conservatives, who feel it should be by the individual who produced it. David Callahan, author of *The Givers*, puts it this way: "Why, he asks, should a collection of philanthropists possess the influence to determine the diseases and medical conditions studied by scientists or choose the art of music the public view or hears?" He would rather the **surplus** be transferred to the government via taxes so that those functions could be accomplished by the National Institutes of Health and the National Endowment for the Arts. Callahan sees philanthropic distribution as power and the ability to influence societal issues such as education, the environment, criminal justice reform, or LGBT rights."[104]

The proprietary aspect of the capitalist system, which produces the most goods of any economic system, is the sanctity of private property including the **surplus** generated. This is the incentive that drives personal effort and innovation. It has been demonstrated that too much wealth transfer by the government through taxation can be self-defeating by lowering the incentive to produce. Alternatively, any economic system will only perpetuate if it reflects the social justice expected by its members. Most people see room for improvement in the current capitalist system as practiced in the United States.

---

[104] Michael Moritz, "Modern Medicis," *Wall Street Journal*, May 3, 2017, A13.

The question remains whether social economic justice is best achieved through confiscatory taxes and government distribution or changing the hearts of the wealthy to distribute in accordance with God's directives? Maximizing government distribution carries the risk of destroying the incentive that makes the **surplus** possible. Relying solely on personal philanthropy you risk *plutogenics* and insufficient distribution. The reality is that nonbelievers make up the majority of what Augustine would call the earthly city which we live in. As a consequence, a social compact to provide a safety net for the less fortunate through a progressive tax system seems appropriate. On the other hand, a broader and healthier distribution is necessary for both the wealthy and the needy to provide for their spiritual and material welfare. President George H. Bush put it this way in 1988:

> For we're a nation of community, of thousands and tens of thousands of ethnic, religious, social, business, labor union, neighborhood, regional and other organizations, all of them varied, voluntary and unique … a brilliant diversity spreads like stars, like a thousand points of light in a broad and peaceful sky. Does government have a place? Yes. Government is part of the nation of communities, not the whole, just a part.[105]

The other part of the nation alluded to by the president is the generous community of the faithful. Those who reflect the fruits of the spirit and are called to distribute beyond what is required by the law.

Looking at capitalism through the exegetical model, where **production - consumption = surplus**, we can see the prodigious productivity that distinguishes it. In fact, the amount of production continues to establish historical highs year after year. No other system comes close. This amount of production tends to run the engine "rich" with excessive buildup and smoke. By this I mean that consumption is supported past what people need for sustenance leading to consumption for consumption's sake.

This is not good for our spiritual health. Although the capitalist system provides the greatest surpluses known to humankind, the surpluses could be even greater without the marketing for contrived needs and conspicuous

---

[105] George H. W. Bush, Address Accepting the Presidential Nomination at the Republican National Convention in New Orleans, 1988.

consumption. The gigantic **surplus** already in capitalist hands requires immediate improvement in its distribution. This will happen only if individuals become involved to fine-tune it through spirit-filled hearts. The distribution of an even greater **surplus** may have to await the Parousia, at which time consumption will become more circumspect.

In the meantime, we will depend on our pastors to soften hearts and inculcate them with the Holy Spirit. We can conclude that scripture does not argue for or against certain positive or normative systems of economics. The scriptures outline an exegetical economic model that we can use to compare various positive economic systems.

But God at this point has left the human function to the free will of humans. That means their frailties still operate and control the production, consumption, and **surplus**. Optimal execution of the Exegetical Economic Model will await divine management.

LOVE THY NEIGHBOR

Sensitivity to social issues and needs is a core message of the love and righteousness in the New Testament. Jesus dealt with the poor, disenfranchised, widowed, and infirm on a person-to-person basis. He made them whole through his unlimited power and **surplus**. He calls on disciples to do the same—heal the sick, right injustice, and reclaim the disenfranchised through individual effort and gifts of **surplus**.

We first look at our neighbor's need in our very own communities. Do they need food? Clothes? Shelter? All of these needs call for solutions. They cannot be addressed without **surplus**. **Surplus** moves typically from individuals to a church, charity, or food bank. It is in the form of checks and clothes. The charities supply items directly to those in need. Such shorter-term needs have been going on for years. But the church has become more involved in longer-term solutions such as jobs and housing. This is empowering giving as opposed to dependency giving. As the church has evolved from a paternal model of religious supervisors to a more egalitarian model of a priesthood of believers, its charity is aimed at less repetitive and more enabling giving. This recognizes that God has given innate gifts to everyone, which will bring them much joy if employed. This new empowering giving has been made possible because of a change in the way the church looks at **surplus** and the wealthy who create and manage it. "Today, in many Christian circles, wealth is seen as anything but a gift to steward well. I find this unfortunate, because I am persuaded that the Augustinian view is the conclusion best supported by scripture. Indeed, I believe material wealth is a gift rather than a curse."[106]

This new emphasis and articulation of wealth allows churches such as the Episcopal Church of the Resurrection in Alexandria, Virginia, to find revitalization in using the capital tied up in its old building to finance 113 units of affordable housing while right-sizing their new church building. A number of churches in North Carolina are addressing the problem of housing locally, regionally, and globally. Members of Myers Park Presbyterian Church are currently working to assist Habitat Charlotte with the construction of multifamily housing while also providing leadership in the construction of a house on a school campus.[107]

Christ Community Covenant Church of Arvada, Colorado, joined with Hearts 'n' Hands to provide prevocational training and continued education to adults with disabilities.[108] Such a focus of charity lifts people from inhibiting circumstances and to rejoin the community as self-supporting creators of **surplus**.

But what of the social issues we become aware of through an increasingly connected world? The faces and issues that enter our homes through the television and internet speak to our hearts. Many churches and NGOs have developed ministries and services to meet those needs through raising and disbursing **surplus**. **Surplus** can travel at the speed of light to any corner of the world simultaneously changing from the currency of the country that sent it to the currency of the country receiving it. It instantly becomes legal tender for food, medicine, and support for the receiving country's needy. Those countries that operate under the economic system of capitalism generate the world's largest surpluses and provide the greatest share of relief to those suffering in other countries. Such capitalist countries also provide the greatest amounts of **surplus** for international cooperation at every level. Many times, countries provide **surplus** directly to other countries called "aid." The greatest amounts of aid originate in countries with advanced capitalist economies.

---

[106] Tom Nelson, *The Economics of Neighborly Love: Investing in Your Community's Compassion and Capacity* (Downers Grove: IVP Books, 2017), 35.

[107] Jose Luis Villasenor, "Affordable Housing—Proper 8," *Strength in Unity, Peace through Justice*, https://www.ncchurches.org/lectionary-archive/year-c/affordable-housing-proper-8/, accessed 2017.

[108] "Hearts 'N' Hands Work Enrichment" (2014).

But what about universal needs that are not bounded by national borders, needs that the citizens of every country require—including a peaceful and healthy environment in which to flourish? That is the environment of the Kingdom of God which Christians are called on to emulate here "on earth as it is in heaven." But the earth is made up of a diverse polity of nations—none of which reflects a Christendom, a government with Christ at the head.

Many mistake the United States to be a Christian nation because it was founded primarily by Christians who had a foundational belief in the Bible. But the founders saw the need to form a country based on freedom—not based on a specific religion. That freedom not only protects religious worship but also private property. It is that freedom that has allowed many to follow Christ and protected a marketplace that has generated the greatest **surplus** in history. God's Kingdom ultimately grows without respect to national boundaries or even freedom. But Christian tap roots buried deep in lands of freedom and capitalism have built the greatest capacity to balm international wounds and address injustice in the world. Can active Christians have an impact in such a free country with a huge economic **surplus**?

Augustine of Hippo addressed that very question in his tome, *The City of God*, written in the late fifth century. He spoke about two cities (polities) living in an integrated fashion, but only one guided by scripture. The secular city he called the City of Man, and the church he called the City of God. The church he refers to is not perfectly replicated by the visible church because believers and nonbelievers are found within and without its walls. The true church is an invisible church known only to God.

> There are no visible, sociological institutions that demarcate the saved from the damned: only God can make that judgment. In our secular age, both pagan Rome and the Christian Church are irreducibly mixed societies. What this means is that, in their temporal dimension, both the political community and the Christian Church are secular: they both depend upon a common set of temporal goods.[109]

The temporal goods, or goods of this world, that he speaks to are the ingredients found in production, consumption, and **surplus**. That is to say

---

[109] Richard Oliver Brooks and James Bernard Murphy, *Augustine and Modern Law* (Farnham: Ashgate, 2011), xvii.

that both the City of Man and the City of God practice the human function $f(h)$. But many feel he is also referring to the spiritual goods of justice, security, and peace.[110]

Augustine would encourage, and even mandate, cooperation between the City of God and the City of Man on such issues—national defense, international justice, and the world's environment. But those who believe in God must also reflect their beliefs in such cooperation. The role of God is the major actor in such issues and humans play a role in his plan. Progressive humanist ideas include that humankind controls the earth's climate and that reduced tensions are best served by unilateral disarmament. These ideas are not biblically supported. This is not to say that mutual armament reductions are not to be sought and that they won't eventually allow us to "beat [our] swords into plowshares" as Isaiah 2:4 tells us. But Isaiah critically points to the action of God in that ultimate outcome.

The first principle of God's economics was stated as $C_v = \beta_0 + \beta_1 f(h)_i + G_i$. Clearly, it demonstrates a direct connection of the human function $f(h)$ to the vitality of the creation. Threats to such vitality include pollution and other byproducts of human production. All kinds of poisons have been freely disbursed into the environment without remediation. Some of the most publicized have been mercury, arsenic, plastic, fluorocarbons, and carbon dioxide. There are many more pollutants beside these. That is because producers have historically not included the cost of remediation in their products thereby offering them for sale at cheaper prices. This issue must be approached internationally by penalizing a bad actor willing to let its citizens live in unhealthy environments so that they can be the low-cost producer of a particular product. Christians should actively engage in "full costing" of products and improved methods of production with cleaner energy.

But there is a caution here. For political purposes, humanists can rouse sentiment to hysterical levels championing reactions with very poor outcomes. Climate warming—its rate and extent—is not universally agreed by supposedly dispassionate scientists. And yet, political alarmists are absolutely convinced that is entirely caused by humans. They point to melting ice caps and potentially submerging coastal towns as a result of humans stoking car and industrial engines with carbon based fuels. (They must suppose the previous ice ages were a result of not feeding the campfires sufficiently at night.) But this is a serious subject and Christians need to understand the

---

[110] Ibid.

urgency of cleaner technologies to fuel our cars and produce our goods. But as a former instructor pilot of a supersonic jet, I can attest to the fact that all thrust and no azimuth will burn all your **surplus** (fuel), getting you very quickly to a place you had no intention of being.

Human hubris in such matters can cause unhelpful outcomes. In his book, *Cool It*, Bjorn Lomborg says that an immediate, hysterical proposal from one politician "for a $140 carbon tax would hike gas prices by $1.25 per gallon, cut the U.S. emissions by half in 2015, yet have an almost immeasurable impact on temperatures—decreasing the average temperature in 2100 by 0.2°F. And the cost would be a dramatic $160 billion annually for the rest of the century."[111]

Additionally, he points to his progressive country of Denmark's quick response initiative to global warming which "will be to postpone global warming by the end of the century by five days at a cost of $300 billion," and a net effect on lives saved, agriculture, and wetlands of $.005 for every $15 million spent.[112] This is in a world where millions face immediate disease, natural disasters, and starvation. Politicians who seek **surplus** to exert power are not always the best stewards of that **surplus**. Stores of **surplus** such as the Gates Foundation, funded by particularly productive entrepreneurs such as Bill Gates and Warren Buffett, show equal gifts in their disbursement effectiveness of those funds.

God's *kairos* (seasonal) time is not always our *chronos* (chronological) time. Thinking more in God's terms, we might train sons and daughters in new industries rather than throw their parents into poverty and despair by abruptly outlawing legacy industries. We might improve our security through mutual arms modifications and not through failing to protect against countries challenging our freedom. It is within Christian understanding, motivation, and sensitivity to balance such rates of change for the good of humanity and a vital creation.

---

[111] Bjørn Lomborg, *Cool It: The Skeptical Environmentalist's Guide to Global Warming*, 1st Vintage Books ed. (New York: Vintage Books, 2008).
[112] Ibid.

CONCLUSION AND IMPLICATIONS

Command those who are rich in this present world
not to be arrogant nor to put their hope in wealth,
which is so uncertain, but to put their hope in God,
who richly provides us with everything for our enjoyment.
Command them to do good, to be rich in good deeds,
and to be generous and willing to share.

—1 Timothy 6:17–18 (NIV)

Jesus did not try and make it hard to understand his teachings. Sometimes humans feel that their lives and the society they live in are so complex that the teachings are difficult to apply. Maybe using the economic tools that we use in our complex economy today will make those teachings obvious again.

People experience the abundant life and more joy the more they understand God's plan for them and align themselves with it. The optimism, dedication, and assurance they display each day make them wonderful members of the church. A church, with Christ as its head, cares and shares with its neighbors and is a protector of the creation.

Christians who look to the Bible for life guidance appreciate the tools and commentaries of others in helping them discern God's meaning. Very few commentaries apply the discipline of economics to that endeavor. But the need has been pointed out by comments such as

> God is interested in all of his creation, both spiritual and material. We know this because of what God tells us about his own opinion and care for the material world.[113]

---

[113] Ritenour, xi.

Economic life raises important social and moral questions for each of us and, for society as a whole. Like family life, economic life is one of the chief areas where we live out our faith, love our neighbor, confront temptation, fulfill God's creative design and achieve our holiness.[114]

People in business who take their cues primarily from economics are deprived of a language system for discussing values, ethical norms, and spiritual principles that relate to what they do ... modern business is largely without a nuanced vocabulary to deal with its own moral potentialities and limitations.[115]

Postponed for years by both theologians and economists who saw no such relevance, the body of bridge literature intertwining both disciplines is beginning to grow. Models from exegetical economics provide common ground for pastors and congregations to celebrate their diversified gifts to build the Kingdom of God. Those that have the gift of **surplus** creation need to be encouraged and celebrated for their gift in the same way that great preachers and talented musicians are appreciated.

Leaders of the church are coming to recognize that economic **surplus** is an indispensable ingredient in kingdom building. They learn this because God has provided a systematic economic model. It is big, broad, and bold. In its simplicity, it subsumes all human models created to describe and understand issues of lesser scope with more complexity. The first theorem,

$$C_v = \beta_0 + \beta_1 f(h) + G_i,$$

shows our relationship to the creation and our requirement to keep it vital. The second theorem,

$$f(h) = production - consumption = surplus,$$

explains the human function to be one of diligent productivity, necessary

[114] Max L. Stackhouse, *On Moral Business: Classical and Contemporary Resources for Ethics in Economic Life* (Grand Rapids: W. B. Eerdmans Pub., 1995), 436.
[115] Ibid., 17.

consumption, and prayed-for **surplus**. Each of these human activities is accomplished through interactivity with the creation and other humans. The Bible, with the elucidation of Jesus, provides very clear instruction on how that interactivity is to take place.

IMPLICATIONS OF EXEGETICAL ECONOMICS

God does not provide revelation on theology and economics to make us more knowledgeable and award us scholarly degrees. He provides that revelation to direct and drive our actions here on earth. Theology treats all of the big three questions: Where do we come from, where are we going, and what do we do in the meantime? It is the final question that economics joins theology to address.

Theology has taken the lead in guiding us in life's purpose. There is a theological body of work entitled "already, but not yet" that has expanded in recent years. It is based on the understanding that Jesus Christ's arrival and mission initiated the Kingdom of God on Earth. However, the Kingdom of God also awaits his return to be recognized and worshipped in its full and complete glory. A key component of this theology is that disciples of Jesus are *already* participants in that kingdom, enjoying its promises and fulfilling its mission. N.T. Wright, a guiding light in this theology, explains it this way:

> Easter was when Hope in person surprised the whole world by coming forward from the future into the present. The ultimate future hope remains a surprise ... leaving us to guess that the reality will be far greater, [while] ... our task in the present ... is to live as resurrection people in between Easter and the final day, with our Christian life, corporate and individual, in both worship and mission, as a sign of the first and a foretaste of the second.[116]

Mission is the word the church uses to describe the Great Commission. "[19] Therefore go and make disciples of all nations, baptizing them in the name of the Father and of the Son and of the Holy Spirit, [20] and teaching them to

---

[116] Wright, 29–30.

obey everything I have commanded you."[117] It is understood that we will do this as disciples of Jesus leaving hope, charity and justice in our wake.

Leslie Newbigin, a leading thinker in Christian theology and missionary work, says, "The church is not meant to call men and women out of the world into a safe religious enclave but to call them out in order to send them back as agents of God's kingship."[118]

The necessity and urgency of mission can be adequately explained theologically, but economic terms are required to explain how it will be specifically implemented. It has to be brought from the macro theological level to the micro level of individual action. Albert Winseman talks on the micro level about the individual morphing from "doing church" to "being church."

> Finding the right fit for people in their congregations—helping them do what they do best—is not just a nice, charitable idea with far-flung ethereal consequence. It's a practical management objective that is powerfully linked to outcomes that are good for the congregation. Those who strongly agree that they have the opportunity to do what they do best in their churches also volunteer more hours of service in their communities and are far more likely to invite others to participate in their churches.[119]

It is a premise of this book that God gave some the "Joseph gift." "What they do best" is to build **surplus**. They do this in a complex way involving skills of productivity and consumption. The opportunity for today's pastor is build their perceived value in the pearl of great price. By investing in that pearl, they become personally engaged with their skills and **surplus** in ministries of hope and justice.

The danger is that the people with the "Joseph gift" operate in a very corrosive and toxic atmosphere to the soul. They are particularly prone to *plutogenics*—the wealth disease. It has various symptoms such as greed,

---

[117] Matthew 28: 19–20 (NIV).

[118] Lesslie Newbigin, *The Open Secret: An Introduction to the Theology of Mission*, 2nd rev. ed. (London: SPCK, 1995).

[119] Albert L. Winseman, *Growing an Engaged Church: How to Stop "Doing Church" and Start Being the Church Again* (New York: Gallup Press, 2007).

arrogance, and separation. Many souls die from this disease. In order for them to be healthy contributors to the body of Christ their spiritual health must be monitored and attended to by their pastor and brothers and sisters in Christ. And there has never been a more opportune time for the **surplus** they manage to be directed for God's purpose.

The Federal Reserve reported that wealth in the United States reached $88.1 *trillion* in 2016, and it is still growing.[120] A very large portion of that **surplus** is controlled and distributed by baby boomers (born 1946–1964). Never before in history have so many people been in charge of distributing such a large **surplus**. These people are retiring and becoming more in control of their time. They are actively making **surplus** distribution decisions. They also have more time to contemplate the big three questions of life. The priceless opportunity to know God and live with him forever is before them. **Surplus** is the vehicle to bring joy into their lives by making them missional, and I believe part of God's plan. I believe that the "already, but not yet" theology of the expanding Kingdom on earth requires a continuous state of **surplus**, making their gifts anticipated and indispensable.

A healthy Christian is joined in Christ without whom they can do nothing. But connected, they can be used as a conduit of faith, hope, and charity. Those with the Joseph gift will also be a conduit of **surplus**. They will give, not because they are taxed or forced to, but because they have Jesus in their heart. Rick Warren reminds us, "You can give without loving, but you cannot love without giving. ... Love means giving up—yielding my preferences, comfort, goals, security, money, energy, or time for the benefit of someone else".[121]

---

[120] Kerry Close, "Americans' Total Wealth Reaches Record High," *Money*, June 9, 2016.
[121] Warren, loc. 1765, Kindle.

EPILOGUE

Then Jesus said, "Whoever has ears to hear, let them hear."

—Mark 4:9 (NIV)

The teachings of Jesus transforms lives for those that call him Lord and Savior. This is how the prologue may have developed.

Sunday has come and gone. Pastor John is on his day off and decompressing after a full-throated effort to "feed his sheep." It was a different kind of message and approach than he had ever given before. The senior pastor had given him a book to read that changed his perspective on **surplus** creation and the wealthy that manage it. His sermon title had been "Glory in the Workplace." And he had opened it up by saying, "I am humbled by what you accomplish each day by going to work. Collectively, you produce more **surplus** and come into contact with more people than I could ever hope to. My gifts are different than yours. I feel like a football coach, proud of his team. You block, run, pass, and leave everything on the field for the glory of God. I so value my role on this team. Let's celebrate and put a team plan together on how God would have us use the **surplus** he has blessed us with."

The service complete, the congregation had exited and shook his hand with nice things to say about his words. He had learned that he might never know how he directly impacted all of their lives—that was in God's hands. But he did make a note to visit with Martin and Anita this week as he had become aware of their challenges. Other developments would take place without his knowing.

Jan and Jerry reflected on the sermon and how they were able to create the **surplus** they now managed. They decided to make a plan using the model **productivity - consumption = surplus**. Since they were both retired their productivity would have to come from the management of the **surplus** they estimated to be around $4,000,000. Their financial advisor indicated they could conservatively plan on a 5 percent annual return of $200,000 on those assets. They looked at their annual living expenses including travel, taxes, and giving and found they almost matched their income. They wanted to give half of their estate to the church and half to their children. The unknown was their future health expenses. So, they decided that they would hold on to the major portion of their estate but start to disburse one half of the church's allotment ($1,000,000) according to an RMD (required minimum disbursement) table designed by the IRS for contributory IRAs. That way they could be active givers and participate in the projects they supported. The initial amount turned out to be $43,668.12 and would stay in that ballpark for the next ten years before starting to decrease. Wow! They decided to explore which church opportunities would give them the greatest blessing for their involvement. They still led active lives. Maybe it was overseas mission work! They were about to enter in to one of the most exciting seasons of their life—praise God!

Sharon also decided to makes some plans using the **production − consumption = surplus** model. She was talented and ambitious, which was reflected in her new job, with a $150,000 annual salary. Sure, she could spend it all, plus some, as some of her new acquaintances were doing. But God told her she should think bigger and bolder. She decided that she would open a Roth IRA in addition to her company retirement plan. She would make maximum annual contributions to both and invest in quality growth stocks. Her financial planner showed that over a thirty-year period with a 9 percent annual tax-free compound return, she could build a multimillion-dollar **surplus**. She was excited and also began a modest but regular commitment to her church. She equated that to a heavenly IRA. She and God were partners in the new plan. He would have a lot to do with how it unfolded.

Anita was excited by the prospect of Pastor John's upcoming visit. She spent so much time volunteering at the church that she saw him quite frequently. This money thing might be too much for her. Maybe Pastor John would be pleased if she told him of her plan to give it all to the poor immediately. She was quite surprised when, during his visit, Pastor John did not think that was what God wanted. He talked to her in terms of productivity, consumption, and **surplus**. He pointed out that her husband purchased the life insurance so that it would provide **surplus** to support her in what she loved to do—serve at the church. Pastor John planned to set her up with a financial planner from the congregation that would be able to help her form a budget and set up automatic pay for her recurring bills. He would also help form a charitable remainder trust to make sure the money would ultimately serve God according to Anita's wishes. She was very relieved that she could look forward to many years of joyful community at her church.

Martin, too, was expecting a visit from Pastor John. But he was not elated. His expectation was for a listening ear and some quiet prayers. Unbeknownst to Martin, Pastor John had already called on the largest management recruiting firm in the community. The president of the firm, who had been prepared to write the anticipated check, was pleasantly surprised when Pastor John said that that was not the purpose of his visit. He had a keen interest in how the business worked and how the president saw it serving the Lord. A warm conversation ensued in which the president explained the contribution to society that his firm's work accomplished. As a part of their mission they sometimes did a bit of *pro bono* work. Thanking Dick for his time, they were now on a first name basis, Pastor John winked and expressed his hope that their next meeting would be at church. Pastor John was filled with anticipation for his visit with Martin. He wanted to help Martin regain his productivity. He was quite confident that was part of God's plan.

Melvin and Louise wistfully looked at the view from their home, enjoying their early evening glass of wine together. They had shared many blessings in their lives, but one was starting to weigh them down. They had generated substantial **surplus** in their lives, and they had learned early what a blessing it was to share it personally for God's purposes. They were staunch and dependable "go-to" people for unexpected church shortfalls. They had raised their children in the church and been active in mission. Now they wanted to be free—free from the earthy responsibilities they had shared as they raised their family. They decided to join a continuing care retirement community (CCRC). Since this was a health contract, it was explained that joining while they could live independently had great advantages. They would stay active in the church and the church would be there for them when they could no longer travel. They looked forward to the peace and joy of this final season of life.

Pastor John sat in his office and reflected on the miracle of the Body of Christ. Just like the human body, its many different parts supported each other. *There can be no higher meaning in life than to serve others for the glory of God*, he thought. And each part, called by God, allowed the body as a whole to live the abundant life—as God intended. He mused on another Pastor John.

That Pastor John, in fact the first one, wrote a letter to his churches (1 John) warning that different kinds of Christianity would be preached in the future. But, he said, only the Christianity that acknowledges Jesus Christ as its Lord and Savior and loves one another can be the true Christianity. The assurance of verse 14, "We know that we have passed out of death into life, because we love the brethren," is conditioned by the question of verse 17: "But whoever has the world's goods, and sees his brother in need and closes his heart against him, how does the love of God abide in him?" (NASB)

The centuries have changed, the question has not. And now it is your turn to answer.

BIBLIOGRAPHY

Augustine, Henry Scowcroft Bettenson, and G. R. Evans. *Concerning the City of God against the Pagans.* New ed. Penguin Classics. London: Penguin, 2003.

Ballor, Jordan J. John Chrysostom. "On Wealth and Poverty, Part 1." In *Acton Institute Powerblog,* 2017. Acton Institute, 2007.

Barclay, William. *The Gospel of Mark.* 2nd ed. Philadelphia: Westminster Press, 1957.

Barker, Kenneth L., ed. *Zondervan Niv Study Bible.* Grand Rapids: Zondervan, 2008.

Barnett, S. J. *The Enlightenment and Religion: The Myths of Modernity.* Manchester: Manchester University Press, 2003.

Bauer, Walter. *A Greek-English Lexicon of the New Testament and Other Early Christian Literature.* Translated by F. Wilbur Gingrich William F. Arndt. 3rd ed., ed. Frederick William Danker. Chicago: The University of Chicago Press, 1957.

Berlin, Adele, Marc Zvi Brettler, Michael A. Fishbane, and Jewish Publication Society. *The Jewish Study Bible.* Oxford: Oxford University Press, 2004.

"Blaise Pascal (1623-1662)," http://www.iep.utm.edu/pascal-b/ - SSH2bv.

Brooks, Richard Oliver, and James Bernard Murphy. *Augustine and Modern Law* Philosophers and Law. Farnham: Ashgate, 2011.

Bruner, Frederick Dale. *The Christbook: A Historical/Theological Commentary.* Waco: Word Books, 1987.

_____. *Matthew: A Commentary.* Vol. 2. Dallas: Word Publishing, 1990.

Bush, George H. W., Address Accepting the Presidential Nomination at the Republican National Convention in New Orleans, 1988.

Close, Kerry. "Americans' Total Wealth Reaches Record High." *Money,* 2016.

The Confession of Faith: Together with the Larger and Lesser Catechismes. London: J. Rothwel, 1658.

Cowley, Robert, Geoffrey Parker, and Society for Military History (U.S.). *The Reader's Companion to Military History.* Boston: Houghton Mifflin, 1996.

Ellicott, Charles John. *Ellicot's Bible Commentary*, ed. Donald N. Bowdle, ThD. Grand Rapids: Zondervan Publishing House, 1971.

Elliot, Elisabeth. *Shadow of the Almighty; the Life & Testament of Jim Elliot.* New York: Harper, 1958.

Evans, Craig A., and Stanley E. Porter. *Dictionary of New Testament Background.* Downers Grove: InterVarsity Press, 2000.

Fea, John. "Religion and Early Politics: Benjamin Franklin and His Religious Beliefs," *Pennsylvania Heritage Magazine* 37, no. 4 (2011).

Fee, Gordon D. *New Testament Exegesis.* 3rd ed. Louisville: Westminster John Knox Press, 2002.

Ferrin, Keith. "We Become What We Worship—Nt Wright." In *Keith Ferrin Blog,* 2017.

Fox, Everett. *The Five Books of Moses : Genesis, Exodus, Leviticus, Numbers, Deuteronomy ; a New Translation with Introductions, Commentary, and Notes.* New York: Schocken Books, 1995.

Geldenhuys, Norval. *Commentary on the Gospel of Luke*. London: Marshall, Morgan and Scott, 1971.

González, Justo L. *Faith and Wealth : A History of Early Christian Ideas on the Origin, Significance, and Use of Money*. 1st ed. San Francisco: Harper & Row, 1990.

Grudem, Wayne A. *Systematic Theology: An Introduction to Biblical Doctrine*. Grand Rapids: Inter-Varsity Press, 1994.

"Hearts 'N' Hands Work Enrichment." 2014.

Heilbroner, Robert L. *Teachings from the Worldly Philosophy*. New York: W. W. Norton, 1996.

Holley, Peter, "Stephen Hawking Just Moved up Humanity's Deadline for Escaping Earth," *The Washington Post*. Accessed 2017. https://www.washingtonpost.com/news/speaking-of-science/wp/2017/05/05/stephen-hawking-just-moved-up-humanitys-deadline-for-escaping-earth/?utm_term=.684a61973b43.

Horsley, Richard A., and John S. Hanson. *Bandits, Prophets & Messiahs: Popular Movements in the Time of Jesus*. Harrisburg: Trinity Press International, 1999.

Irenaeus. *Five Books of S. Irenaeus : Bishop of Lyons, against Heresies* Library of Fathers of the Holy Catholic Church. Oxford: J. Parker, 1872.

King, Martin Luther, Clayborne Carson, and Peter C. Holloran. *A Knock at Midnight : Inspiration from the Great Sermons of Reverend Martin Luther King, Jr*. London: Abacus, 2000.

Lewis, C. S. *The Great Divorce, a Dream*. London: G. Bles, 1945.

_____. *The Complete C.S. Lewis Signature Classics*. 1st ed. San Francisco: HarperSanFrancisco, 2002.

Lomborg, Bjørn. *Cool It : The Skeptical Environmentalist's Guide to Global Warming*. 1st Vintage Books ed. New York: Vintage Books, 2008.

Malthus, T. R. *Additions to an Essay on the Principle of Population*. 1st American ed. Georgetown: C. Cruickshank, 1831.

_____. *An Essay on the Principle of Population* Everyman's University Library. London: J. M. Dent, 1973.

Marr, Holly. "11 Inspiring Quotes from Tim Keller." In *Logos Talk*, 2017: Logos Bible Software, 2016.

Metzger, Bruce M., ed. *The Oxford Companion to the Bible*. Edited by Michael D. Coogan. New York: Oxford University Press, 1993.

Metzger, James A. *Consumption and Wealth in Luke's Travel Narrative*. Leiden: Brill, 2007.

"Misesinstitute Austrian Economics, Freedom, and Peace." https://mises.org/about-mises/what-austrian-economics.

Moore, Michael S. *Wealthwatch: A Study of Socioeconomic Conflict in the Bible*. Eugene: Pickwick Publications, 2011.

Moritz, Michael. "Modern Medicis." *Wall Street Journal*, May 3, 2017.

Nelson, Tom. *The Economics of Neighborly Love: Investing in Your Community's Compassion and Capacity*. Downers Grove: IVP Books, 2017.

Neusner, Jacob. *The Economics of the Mishnah*. Chicago: University of Chicago Press, 1990.

_____. *The Mishnah: Social Perspectives: Philosophy, Economics, and Politics*. Leiden: Brill, 1999.

New American Standard Bible. Study ed. Philadelphia: A. J. Holman, 1976.

Newbigin, Lesslie. *The Open Secret : An Introduction to the Theology of Mission*. 2nd rev. ed. London: SPCK, 1995.

Newton, Isaac. Two Notable Corruptions of Scripture, Bishop Horsley, Watchmaker Publishing.

Nouwen, Henri J. M. *The Return of the Prodigal Son*. New York: Doubleday, 1994.

_____. "The Spirituality of Fund-Raising." In *Henri Nouwen Society*, ed. Estate of Henri J. M. Nouwen. Richmond Hill: Upper Room Ministries, 2004.

Peterson, Eugene H. *Tell It Slant: A Conversation on the Language of Jesus in His Stories and Prayers*. Cambridge: Wm B. Eerdmans Publishing Co, 2008.

Radmacher, Earl D. Th.D., ed. *The Nkjv Study Bible*. Nashville: Thomas Nelson, Inc., 2007.

Ramanathan, Marcelo Sanchez Sorondo and Veerabhadran. "Pursuit of Integral Ecology." *Science*, May 13, 2016, 862.

Ritenour, Shawn. *Foundations of Economics: A Christian View*. Eugene: Wipf and Stock Publishers, 2010.

Saggi, Rupi, "Why Study Economics?" Vanderbilt College of Arts and Science. Accessed 2017. https://as.vanderbilt.edu/econ/undergraduate/why-study-economics.php.

Sider, Ron. "The Holy Calling of Wealth Creation Isn't So Simple." *Christianity Today*, August 24, 2017.

Sintern, Cathrin M. van. "The Oxford Declaration on Christian Faith and Economics" (1990): Vorgeschichte, Analyse, Rezeption Und Ausblick." Master's thesis, Oxford Centre for Mission Studies and University of Wales, 2003.

Smith, Adam. *An Inquiry into the Nature and Causes of the Wealth of Nations*, 5th ed. London: A. Strahan, 1789.

Spiegel, Henry William. *The Growth of Economic Thought*. Englewood Cliffs: Prentice-Hall, 1971.

Stackhouse, Max L. *On Moral Business: Classical and Contemporary Resources for Ethics in Economic Life*. Grand Rapids: W. B. Eerdmans Pub., 1995.

Staff, Mayo Clinic, "Nutrition and Healthy Eating," Mayo Clinic. Accessed 2017. https://www.mayoclinic.org/healthy-lifestyle/nutrition-and-healthy-eating/in-depth/gout-diet/art-20048524.

Thaler, Richard H., "Misbehaving: The Making of Behavioral Economics," W. W. Norton & Company.

Tolstoy, Leo. *Essays and Letters*. London: Grant Richards, 1903.

Villasenor, Jose Luis. "Affordable Housing—Proper 8." *Strength in Unity, Peace through Justice*. Accessed 2017. https://www.ncchurches.org/lectionary-archive/year-c/affordable-housing-proper-8/.

Warren, Rick. *The Purpose Driven® Life: What on Earth Am I Here For?* Philadelphia: Running Press Book Publishers, 2003.

_____. "Use This Simple Principle to Manage Your Money Well." In *Pastor Rick's Daily Hope*, 2017.

"Wealth Creation Manifesto," Lausanne Movement. https://www.lausanne.org/content/wealth-creation-manifesto.

Wedgeworth, Steven, "John Calvin on the Use of Goods and Money," The Calvinist International Accessed 2017. http://www.calvinistinternational.com/.

"Why Study Economics?" Washington University in St. Louis. Accessed 2017. https://economics.wustl.edu/undergraduate/whyecon.

"Why Study? Economics," The University of Bristol. Accessed 2017. http://whystudyeconomics.ac.uk/.

Winseman, Albert L. *Growing an Engaged Church: How to Stop "Doing Church" and Start Being the Church Again*. New York: Gallup Press, 2007.

Wright, N. T. *Surprised by Hope*. New York: HarperCollins, 2008.

Zondervan Publishing House (Grand Rapids Mich.). *Nasb Compact Reference Bible: New American Standard Bible*. Grand Rapids: Zondervan Pub. House, 2000.

CPSIA information can be obtained
at www.ICGtesting.com
Printed in the USA
LVHW050856030519
616446LV00001B/1